Basketmaking

Basketmaking

Georgia Crook

The Art of Crafts

First published in 2000 by
The Crowood Press Ltd
Ramsbury, Marlborough
Wiltshire SN8 2HR

British Library Cataloguing-in-Publication Data

A catalogue record for this book is available from the British Library.

ISBN 1 86126 310 4

Typeface used: Melior

Photography by Carolyne Charrington
Designed and typeset by Focus Publishing, Sevenoaks, Kent
Printed and bound by Leo Paper Products, China

Contents

Acknowledgements

Thank you to all the people who have helped in any aspect of the compilation of this book. In particular, I would like to thank the myriad of people who have gone out of their way to boost my confidence as a basketmaker. Specifically I would like to thank Graham Kent for his consideration whilst I was learning the craft of basketmaking and also for his wonderful drawings, which form an integral part of this book. I would like to thank Carolyne Charrington for dashing out to take all the photographs when the sun shone and Inniemore Lodge School of Painting for allowing us to use one of their studios when it didn't! Thanks go to Jane Wilkinson of the Monimail Tower Project for allowing me to confirm my willow propagation facts against her own bits of research and to Lizzie Farey, Trevor Leat and Graham Glanville for contributing photographs and pieces of their work.

Thanks go also to Seth Crook for providing me with yet more useful names and addresses to go at the end of the book. G.C.

Introduction

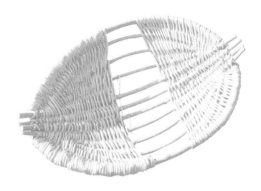

It has been said that humans have an intuitive ability to weave a basket, just as a spider spins a web or a bird makes a nest. Archaeological work indicates that it wasn't long before humans began to make baskets, and ancient texts make frequent references to the industry. Although some contemporary basketry can be much more refined, a good understanding of fundamental weaving principles are clearly there, even in the earliest of baskets. These basic principles remain unchanged today and this book is intended to introduce the beginner to just some of them.

A complete beginner can master the concepts involved in making a simple basket in a very short space of time. As you become more familiar with the techniques, your baskets will get stronger and more symmetrical but even your first attempts can be extremely appealing. Just as early humans did, you can combine as many different materials as can be found in the 'garden', as well as materials that have been specifically grown for the purpose of basketmaking. The projects in this book use traditional willow techniques in combination with what is loosely described as 'hedgerow' material; sometimes collected from anywhere but the hedgerow, from places such as woods, meadows and even the shoreline. The countryside is bursting with potential basketry material. If you have ever noticed the beauty of the buds on the trees or the seed heads on the grasses, now is your chance to usefully bring them into the house by weaving them into a basket!

Basketry is an excellent mentor when discovering the countryside and an excellent outlet for the creative impulse. I have learned more about the cycles and methods of nature than I could have done practising practically any other craft; but you don't have to stick to natural materials. Try using man-made materials such as plastics, synthetic ropes, card or wire. Combine your basketmaking with techniques used in other crafts such as wood-working, macrame, collage or even ceramics. In other words – experiment!

HISTORY

It is difficult to say whether the basketmaking industry ever had a height, but much easier to identify a decline in its importance in Britain and Europe, most prominently in the middle-half of this century when anything that was old or traditional was most definitely out and emerging technologies were busy devising seemingly newer and better replacements. The commonest cliché associated with this decline is that baskets were replaced by plastics, and to a large extent, this is true. However, basketry did somehow manage to maintain a sturdy position in people's affections; even to the extent that plastics manufacturers felt the need to mould their receptacles in a manner that simulated the look of a basket.

Today basketry is also favoured as a result of its environmental sustainability. Comparing the impact of plastics waste with basketry waste is not difficult. There has always been something very reassuring about a well-made basket; it connects us with our past by virtue of its long-standing tradition, and has always been seen as a symbol of reliability and trust-worthiness.

Although the art of making some kinds of regional baskets has now been lost as a result of this downturn in interest; and others have only just survived (for example, the straw 'kishie' of Shetland and the 'oak swill' of the Lake District), basketry is now enjoying a resurgence in favour, and is finding its new place in the modern world. The timeless simplicity and purity of design in the Shaker crafts of America has ensured the survival of the ash-splint basket, which is now experiencing a justified revival.

Being so used to the presence of basketry in our domestic, agricultural and industrial environment, it is now easy to take it for granted. Yet the influence of the basketry industry in the past has certainly been immense. Nearly every village would have had a basketmaker not so long ago; and in some cases the life of whole communities would have revolved around the growth of materials and the production of baskets.

The tradition of cultivating materials for basketmaking is almost as old as the craft itself. In 25BC Strabo, the Greek geographer, commented on the growing of reed for basketmaking. In Britain, as everywhere else, the social culture is riddled with evidence of the industry's previous importance. Have you ever thought where the title for the traditional dance tune Strip-the-Willow comes from? Stripping the willow, when it was in season, was an activity undertaken by everyone. Children were even excused from school to help carry the task out, in much the same way as they were when they were excused for potato picking.

Baskets served every imaginable function, from the fishing creel to the spinner's fleece basket; from the seed lip to the bath chair, ox muzzle and coffin! Most people would be surprised to know that in Britain, basketmakers have had their own professional association since 1569. This is the 'Worshipful Company of Basketmakers', which was given a Royal Charter in 1937. So, even in the sixteenth century there were large numbers of basketmakers whose organization and standards needed to be co-ordinated.

We know that the making of baskets preceded the making of pottery. Archaeologists have discovered shards of neolithic pottery with imprints of basket weave, indicating that the basket was used to mould the pot. The first Christian church at Glastonbury in England is reputed to have been made of wickerwork.

The type and scale of weaving activity in Britain is not easy to analyze due to poor conservation conditions, but in Egypt, where the climate is more conducive to conservation, innumerable artefacts have been found. Granary linings and rushwork chairs in Tut-ankh-Amen's tomb amongst many other things. Archaeological work in the Middle East provides us with hundreds of examples dating back thousands of years. The Romans, just like many modern plastics manu-facturers, gave a woven impression on many of their ceramic storage vessels, presumably either to reassure the purchaser that they were of good quality, or because nobody could imagine a storage vessel that didn't at least look like a basket; and, of course, we mustn't forget the ark of rushes made for Moses!

TRADITION AND DIVERSITY

The interchange of basketry skills and materials probably began as soon as intercontinental trading and travel began thousands of years ago, and basketry is still as open to these multifold global influences today, just as any other medium in contemporary society. At the end of the twentieth century it is increasingly being looked upon as an art form, as well as a time-honoured craft. One reason for this is its tendency to draw upon a wide variety of cultures and traditions when designing form and function. Strict patterns need only be followed when reproducing traditional regional baskets, otherwise

there is no reason not to combine a wide variety of proven techniques when making your own basket. A poorly designed basket is a weak basket, or one that does not fulfil its intended function – not necessarily one that does not stick to the letter of tradition, either in its design or the methods used to manufacture it.

Such a wide array of influences on the contemporary basketmaker has, not surprisingly, engendered a similarly wide ranging school of thought on the subject. Some basketmakers feel it is important to retain the regional purity and integrity of basketmaking by preserving and promoting traditional designs. Others, although real devotees to the utilitarian cause, play around

Cumbrian Oak Swill.

Polish willow potato pannier.

with traditional techniques but contrive new designs, which are immediately relevant to the craft's contemporary purpose. There are also basketmakers who devote themselves to the aesthetic cause and don't actually make functional baskets at all, but use the techniques to make sculptural work. The one thing that unites them all, however, is an innate affection for the form and texture that basketry displays. It is to the craft's credit that there is such a wide variety of tradition and potential to be exploited.

Different regions and countries have developed their own styles of basketmaking, which optimize the use of the materials that are indigenous to the local area. The Shetland 'Kishie' is made entirely of straw due to the poor supply of woody materials on the islands. The Cumbrian 'Swill', hovers on the line between green woodworking and more conventional basketry (being made of riven oak and hazel), and makes use of the once abundant oak woodland in that area. Hazel was once copp-iced widely all over the British Isles, being used not only for basket-making but, like willow, it was also cropped for many uses such as hurdle making. Alpine farmers in Central Europe still use tough hazel baskets to this day. In the south-eastern region of America it is the white oak frame basket that survives as the emblem of pioneering culture; and no-one can help but marvel at the startling skill and intricacy displayed in the coiled work of the American Indian tradition.

In Britain, willow wood is one of a number of traditional basketmaking materials, which all have their own individual methods of working. Rush is still harvested on rivers such as the Avon today, although on a much smaller scale; it was once a huge industry. In other parts of the world bamboo, cane, flax, birch bark, roots and even seaweed are used to make baskets, imported examples of which we can readily see in our local shops.

1 Materials and Preparation

WILLOW

There are four basic colours of willow that you can buy commercially: brown, black, buff and white. They are supplied in bundles called 'bolts' and can be anything from 1 to nearly 3m in length. It is also possible to buy mixed-length bolts, which is very useful when you are just beginning and only need a small amount of material, or if you don't want or need to make a lot of baskets.

Brown and black willow has been cut and dried with the bark still on the wood. The brown is entirely untreated except for being left to dry, but the black is made by steaming seasoned rods and this gives the bark a very dark brown sheen. Both buff and white have been stripped of their bark, either manually, or commercially by machine. To attain the buff colour, the rods are boiled in their bark; the tannin in the bark staining the wood inside. Stripping the loose bark from the rod reveals the colour. White willow is made while the sap is rising in the spring, just as the rods are beginning to bud. The bark is 'saggier' at this stage and can be easily stripped off revealing an attractive ivory colour. White willow can only be prepared at one time of year and is, therefore, often in very short supply; so unless you are going to grow your own, order your white willow with the commercial dealer early.

Once you have got your bolt of willow you will notice that the rods vary in thickness, even though they may be of approximately equal length, so it is a good idea to sort them out into girth sizes (thickness at the butt): thick, medium and thin. This will save time later, as you will need a different thickness of rod for each part of the basket. Store in a cool, dry place. If you have enough room, cut the ties around the bolt of willow to let the air flow through because buff and steamed willow, in particular, have a tendency to gather mould in damp and airless conditions. Mould will leave an unattractive mottled stain on the rods. This effect can be alleviated on buff rods if you give them a quick dip in a mild bleach solution.

PREPARATION OF WILLOW

Soaking

Unless you are using freshly cut 'green' or 'clung' (half-dried) willow, you must soak it in water and mellow it in order to make it pliable enough to weave. I have a stream running by my house, which I use to immerse my rods in (remembering to tie and weight them down well to guard against flash floods!). If you have no access to this facility then you will have to find some sort of tank to soak the willow rods in. An old bath will do for most purposes, unless you need to soak

Soaking willow.

Opposite: Bolts of willow and collected hedgerow material.

long rods for bigger baskets. I do not recommend using the bath in your own bathroom for this. Not only will you annoy everyone else in the house when they find the willow soaking where they should be, but it will also stain the bath. A cattle trough or some other galvanized tank is ideal. The aim is to completely submerge the willow. Depending on the size and type of willow, it will need soaking anything from an hour to a week. Make sure the rods are completely covered by weighting them down with heavy stones or something similar. The thin ends of the rods will take less time to soak than the thick ends, so just submerge the thin ends towards the end of the soaking process, otherwise they will become oversoaked.

Oversoaking, to which brown and steamed (black) rods are especially susceptible, discolours and weakens the bark. This not only looks unsightly but also makes it difficult to weave the basket without stripping the bark from the wood. Unfortunately it is impossible to indicate exact soaking periods as these will depend on the kind of rods being soaked and the temperature of the water. Only with experience will you be able to estimate more accurately how long your rods should remain soaking. However, there are some general guidelines that will help you guard against under or oversoaking in the first instance.

Unstripped willow takes days to soak, whereas stripped willow only takes a

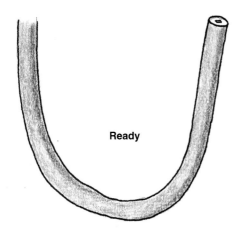

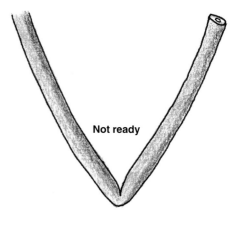

The 'U/V' test.

matter of hours. This may be one explanation as to why so many commercially made baskets are made with unstripped willow. It takes less organization to prepare a batch of buff or white willow than it does to prepare a batch of brown or steamed. Making

Approximate Soaking Times

LENGTH	BUFF/WHITE	BROWN/BLACK
90cm (3ft)	1–2h	2–3 days
120cm (4ft)	2–3h	days
150cm (5ft)	3–4h	4–5 days
180cm (6ft)	3–4h	5–7 days

baskets necessitates soaking a variety of sizes, and if more than one colour is also being used, the soaking process needs to be timed quite carefully.

When the rods are ready, they have an overall darker and fuller appearance, as they will have absorbed a lot of water by now. A helpful way of testing whether your rods are ready is to give it the 'U/V' test. Pick out a butt end from your bundle and gently bend it. If it curves into a 'U' shape then it is ready; if it kinks into a 'V' it is not. Use this test to check the rods at regular intervals until

you get the hang of how the rods should look when they are properly soaked. Try not to get too discouraged if you misjudge soaking for a while. Most of my early baskets were made with undersoaked material and are consequently covered in vast numbers of kinks and jagged edges!

Mellowing

Mellowing is an essential part of willow preparation. Weaving the rods is much easier when the willow has been mellowed and the overall appearance of the finished basket will be vastly improved. Once you think your willow has finished soaking, pull it out of the water and wrap it in dampened sacking, or an old blanket or towel. Buff and white willow should be mellowed for 2–4 hours or overnight before use, while unstripped willow should be left at least a day or two, depending on its size, before use; this makes the willow much more pliable. Unstripped willow can be kept ready to use like this for up to a week but stripped willows will only keep for a couple of days before they start to go mouldy and slimy, in which case use the buff or white rods immediately, or rinse and dry them out in the sun. It is possible to re-soak and use white and buff willows, but you should avoid doing this with brown and black willows, as they will have lost a lot of their original colour and strength.

HEDGEROW MATERIALS

The term 'hedgerow' basketry is loosely used to describe the use of materials that have not been specifically grown for the purpose of basketmaking. The materials can come from the hedgerow but can also be collected from woodlands, gardens, meadows and shorelines. You should look for 'stuff' (as basketmakers call their materials), that is reasonably long, strong and is pliable enough to be bent loosely around the hand. Preferably it should taper from butt to tip. If it fits this description then it is probably worth experimenting with. Look out for climbing and trailing plants, suckers and old pruning sites, remembering to get permission to cut materials when you wander outside your own garden. Most people are happy for their hedges and shrubs to be trimmed if you ask. A word of warning though, whilst most plants thrive on an annual pruning, some can be decimated when cut back, so try and find out what it is you are cutting first!

It is important to keep thickness, strength and pliability constantly in mind when collecting, as different thicknesses of wood are needed for different parts of the basket. Stems of one-year's growth are usually the most suitable for weavers, as they tend to become a little too thick and stiff if they are older than this. Handle bows and side stakes need to be much thicker than weavers, and do not need to be so pliable. Ideally weavers should be no thicker than a pencil. For ease of use, select rods without side-shoots at first, though they can be used quite imaginatively after you have mastered some basic techniques. Trim the side-shoots off if there aren't too many. After the priority of structural necessity comes colour, texture and aroma, and this is where the real fun begins. As long as a few principles, which ensure strength and durability, are followed, you can pretty much do anything you like with whatever materials you find, although you will quickly discover that certain materials lend themselves more easily to different parts of the basket.

Woody Stems

Nearly all woody stemmed hedgerow material should be used when it has had a short time to dry out. Only a few, such as brambles, clematis and elm, can be used immediately. Unlike commercial willow, most woody hedgerow material does not have the virtue of being re-soakable; so only cut as much as you need to use in one season. It should be cut in the winter when the leaves have fallen and the sap is down; and before new spring growth has begun. By the time late spring or early summer arrives much of the material that was cut in the winter will be too brittle to use.

After cutting woody stuff, sort it into sizes, tie it into bundles and label, if necessary, then leave it in a sheltered place outside to 'cling', i.e. the stems are ready when they have lost a lot of their natural moisture but still retain enough pliability for weaving. It will take different types of material different lengths of time to reach this point. Some materials may only take a few days to cling, whereas others may take weeks. Go back and check your bundles of stuff every few days to see how they are progressing. Letting the material dry out a little first is important since, without doing so, large gaps in the weave of the finished basket will develop as the stems dry out and shrink. If by accident the stems have not quite dried out enough

EXAMPLES OF USABLE WOODY MATERIALS

Willows (e.g. *Salix alba, S. daphdoides, S. caprea, S. cinera, S. fragilis*), Dogrose, Dogwood, Holly, Heather root, Jasmine, Elm, Wisteria, Lime suckers, Cotoneaster, Hazel, Ivy, Poplar, Spruce, Mistletoe, Honeysuckle, Alder, Clematis, Birch, Privet, Laurel, Larch, Vine, Mallow, Periwinkle, Buckthorn, Blackthorn, Weeping Cherry, Lilac, Bramble, Beech.

EXAMPLES OF USABLE LEAFY STEMS

Monbretia, Gladioli, Iris, Flax, hay and straw, Sedges, Marram grass, Pampas, Palm, Reedmace, Soft Bog Rush, Cotton grass.

when you weave them, you can cheat by weaving in a couple more bits to fill the gaps. Cheating is a little bit more acceptable in hedgerow work!

Leafy Stems

Leafy material should be collected at the height of the summer to make the most of its strength and colour. Dry the stems out thoroughly before use, as they will shrink substantially. Unlike the woody materials (except willows), they can be stored when dry and used as necessary throughout the year.

Cut as long a length of the stems as possible and spread them out in a dry, dark and airy place, turning occasionally to prevent damp or mouldy patches appearing. I spread mine out across some chicken wire in the roof of my shed but you could also put a few in your airing cupboard if you don't have much space elsewhere. Drying the stems out in the sun is a quick method but a lot of the stem colour is lost this way and you have to be perpetually on guard for any rain showers.

When you are ready to use the leaves, sprinkle them with water from a hose or can. Never soak them because this makes them brittle. Wrap them in a damp cloth for a couple of hours or overnight, they will then be ready for use. The same preparation procedure is applied to commercially bought rush. Only dampen as much as you need, as the material won't last long like this before it starts to go slimy. It is possible to use hay and straw stems by quickly dipping them in hot water before use.

Some More Materials

RUSH

The bulrush *Scirpus lacustris* provides the material for most rushwork chair-seating and basketry. It grows in slow-moving rivers and is harvested in mid-late summer. Rush grows up to 2m in height and is very smooth textured and pliable. It is sold and despatched in bundles in much the same way that willow is.

BARK

Bark can be used both for basketry and chair-seating. It is stripped from the 'bast' (i.e. the inner bark) of trees such as whych elm, sycamore and hemlock, using a draw knife. The native American tradition uses large folded and sewn sheets of various hardwood bark to make baskets.

SEAGRASS AND CORD

Seagrass can be purchased in naturally coloured corded hanks. It is made from sedges gathered in the Far East and is usually used as a chair-seating material. Other cords are available, which use a variety of different materials, for example, polypropylene, flax and hemp.

CANE

Cane is derived from a creeper of the rattan family, which grows in many parts of the world from Africa to China but is imported mainly from the South East Asia region. The outer part is usually used for materials for chair-seating and the processed inner bark is used for basketry. It is sold by weight and comes in a variety of sizes.

RAFFIA

Raffia is a derivative of the leaf bast of the raffia palm and can be bought in naturally coloured or dyed hanks. It is extremely long, strong and supple, and is most commonly used in coiled basketry work where it is wrapped around a core.

DYEING MATERIALS

Most of the materials mentioned can be successfully dyed; willow, cane, seagrass and raffia taking colour particularly well. Any generally available dye designed for use on natural materials will do, although its also worth experimenting with the natural dyes that can be derived from the plant materials surrounding us in the countryside. Following the manufacturer's instructions or other traditional recipes for dyeing, place small coiled quantities of your basket material in a pan or bucket, and larger quantities in a length of plugged drainpipe. Any commercially available woodstain can also be successfully used.

Alternative basketry materials.

2 Willow Propagation

Willows are a favourite of basketmakers for good reasons. The rods are extremely tough and pliable, both when they are green and when they have been seasoned and re-soaked. They are easy and quick to grow, coppice and crop in large quantities. There are also huge numbers of varieties that have different working qualities and are therefore suitable for making a range of different kinds of baskets. Willows belong to the family *Salicaceae* of which there are over three hundred *Salix* species growing all over the habitable world, mainly in the northern temperate regions. Some grow into tall graceful trees such as Weeping Willows, others such as Goat Willow have a short and shrubby habit, whilst some are positively prostrate, creeping low over the ground. In Britain the smallest species to be found is the appropriately named 'Least Willow' (*Salix herbacea*), which grows to only 1 or 2cm in height, and the largest is the White Willow (*S. alba*), which can grow to 25 or 30m in height. Trying to identify willows though can sometimes be extremely tricky since they hybridize extensively.

Willow rods for weaving can always be bought from a dealer to mix and provide the framework for your other materials. The numbers and varieties grown on a commercial scale, however, are really quite limited, so it's a good idea if you have a spare corner in your garden to plant a few of your own. Willows are very quick and easy to grow and even the cultivation of one or two varieties can make all the difference to your baskets.

They can provide excellent windbreaks and shelterbelts for the most delicate parts of the garden and can even be planted in areas thought to be unworkable, although this is not ideal if you want to grow a good productive crop. In Britain, the varieties most suitable for basketmaking trad-itionally occur on the deep richer soils of the lowland areas, but I have had success growing basket willows in the most inhospitable of territories – so don't let this stop you experimenting and finding out which varieties best suit your location.

All kinds of willows can be used in baskets but there are three varieties that are considered to be most suitable: Common Osier (*S. viminalis*), Almond Willow (*S. triandra*) and Purple Willow (*S. purpurea*). *Salix triandra* is the most commonly grown commercial variety, so it may be more worthwhile at first to grow a few varieties that are not already supplied by the willow farms. All these species have different working qualities and can fulfil a different role in the working of your basket. Propagation of willows is difficult to achieve from seed and cuttings are usually used as a result. Use 1–3-year-old spring cuttings are used of approximately pencil thickness and about 25–30cm long. You can plant them randomly and decoratively around your garden, or try growing your own 'holt'. A holt is what basketmakers call their osier beds, which can be as small as just a few rows of willows. Commercially, the sets are put in at sufficient distances to allow the passage of machinery during harvesting, but one can put them in closer together at

Opposite: Young willow stool showing early growth.

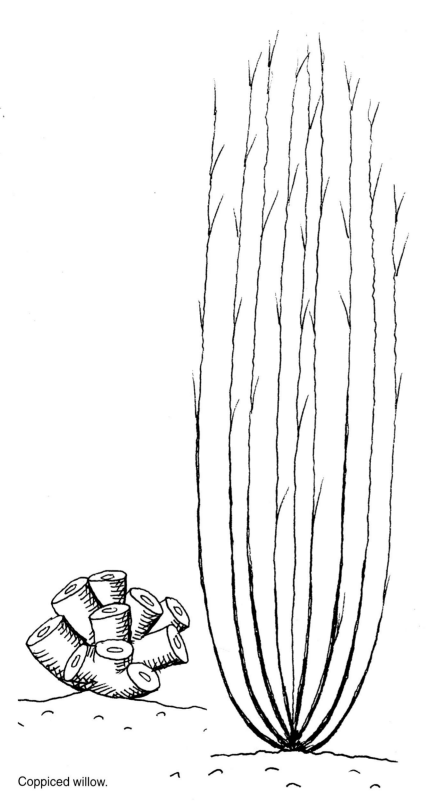

Coppiced willow.

around 50–60cm apart. Make a slit with a spade and push the cutting in vertically, leaving two or more buds (6–8cm) above the surface of the soil. Remember to put the cutting in the right way up (i.e. with the buds facing upwards)! Your cutting will respond well to good soil preparation. Willows can tolerate a lot but they don't thrive in excessive shade or soils that are very acidic or boggy; though they will tolerate occasional flooding. Weeds also pose a significant problem for young willows, which can be quickly smothered until they have put on significant growth. Put down black plastic to act as a mulch to counteract the problem, if you don't feel you will be able to keep well on top of the weeding.

Unless your willows are attacked by pests or disease, which can prompt side-shoots and rust spots on the bark (planting a group of mixed varieties will help to counteract this), the willows can be more or less left to romp away; but they must be kept weed-free for the first three years at least. Weeds will smother the emergence of the delicate buds, which appear from below the surface of the soil around the trunk stem. Be careful not to knock off these hidden buds when weeding in the spring and early summer. Traditionally, commercial farms grazed cows in the willow beds if there was a danger of frost, allowing them to eat the sensitive growing tips and thus preventing the frost damage that would delay progress in the growing season. If you think there is a danger of frost, give the stumps or 'stools' a light mulch. Fertilizing is unnecessary, since this is provided each winter by the leaf fall. Willows can be phenomenally tough. I once had delivery of some freshly cut willow sticks, remaining after a friend had pollarded a large *S. viminalis*. After cutting off all the rods I needed for my baskets, I threw the rather large stump that was left over onto the wood pile, expecting it to season and be ready to burn on the wood stove the following summer. In the spring, however, it began to throw out shoots, so I pressed the base of the stump an inch into the soil of my garden. It is now a very healthy and attractive feature there, and year on year provides me with plenty of material for my baskets.

It will take 3–5 years to start getting a really good basketmaking crop from your willows, and involves coppicing or pollarding them in the winter. Traditionally, this cutting back was done with a billhook but if there are only a few to cut, a pair of secateurs and a small pruning saw should suffice. To coppice willows, cut all the rods as close to the ground as you can, using nice clean sloping cuts and leaving no ragged edges. This will prevent the base of the plant trapping water and starting to rot. The established root system then encourages each stem to multiply the number of rods it produces on the following year's growth. Cutting can be carried out any time before the sap rises and the leaves begin to emerge. Once the rods are cut, sort them into sizes and types and leave then in a sheltered spot to dry out for a few weeks, turning them occasionally to ensure even drying.

WILLOW VARIETIES USEFUL FOR BASKETRY

SALIX VIMINALIS

S. viminalis is vigorous and hardy. Its rods are thicker than *S. triandras* or *S. purpureas* and have more pith and an abrupt taper. It can grow 1.5–3m per annum and is, therefore, more suitable for large or sturdy working baskets. Examples are: Gigantin, Mullatin, Refenwede, Black Satin, Wisendra, Gallica, Stone Osier, Brown Merrin.

SALIX PURPUREA

S. purpurea is usually hardier than *S. triandras*. It is valued for its attractively coloured barks and catkins. It has delicate, slender rods and is consequently ideal for fine basketry. Purpureas can grow 1–1.5m annually. Examples are: Dicky Meadows, Lancashire / Leicestershire Dicks, Green Dicks, Dark Dicks, Brittany Greens, Abbeys, Welsh, Jagielonka.

SALIX TRIANDRA

S. triandra, in particular Black Maul, is the most commonly grown commercial crop. *S. triandra* is most frequently used to make white and buff willow. It has less pith than other varieties and a gentle taper, being called 'Fine Tops' traditionally. A good all rounder, *S. triandra* can be used in many different ways to make most sizes of baskets. It grows up to 1.5–2.5m annually. Examples are: Black Maul, Whissender, Stone Rod, Sweet Willow, Newkind, Blacktop, Sarda, Norfolk, Grisette, French, Spaniardia.

SALIX DAPHNOIDES

S. daphnoides tends to have deep red and purple bark and rather attractive catkins, and is not usually commercially grown for basketry purposes. It can grow up to 8m in height. Examples are: Continental Purple, Black Willow, Oxford Violet, Aglaia.

SALIX ALBA

S. albas can grow into large trees but is still useful in basketry when coppiced. It has an attractive range of bark ranging from red to yellow. Examples are: Vitellina Nova, Chermesina, Britzensis, Liempde, Malontelelo.

3 Workshop, Tools and Techniques

By its definition as a handcraft, basketry needs only a few simple tools, and unless you begin to explore a very specialized area of the craft, most of the tools are readily available. Certainly the tools required for all the projects in this book will meet your needs for quite some time to come.

TOOLS: THE BASIC SET

SECATEURS

A good sharp pair of secateurs is essential. Remember you will be using them a lot more than the average pair was designed for, so try to get a pair you can sharpen and that have metal handles, as plastic handles tend to break with intensive use.

KNIFE

Any good strong handknife will do in the first instance. Craft knives are OK as a very temporary measure but you will find the thinness of the blade a hindrance, so try and find a knife with a good sturdy blade. The handknife is used at many stages of the basketmaking process.

BODKIN

A bodkin is a sharp conical-shaped tool used for creating gaps in the weave and piercing rods in squarework. They are made in various sizes and can be obtained from a specialist supplier; or if you know a metal worker, have them make one up for you. A small bodkin of about 19mm in length should be adequate for most needs. You can improvise a bodkin till you manage to get hold of the real thing by filing down a screwdriver, for instance.

RAPPING IRON

A rapping iron is a band of heavy metal used for tapping down the weave as you work the sides of the basket. Again, irons designed for the purpose can be bought from a specialist dealer but they can be quite easily contrived by using a tyre leaver, for example.

SCREWBLOCK

A screwblock is used to weave the bases of squarework. You can't really buy them but this is because they are so simple to make. Cut two pieces of 50–50cm timber to approximately 40cm in length. Drill two holes about 10cm from the ends of each, big enough to fit a coach bolt through, and secure with wing nuts.

WEIGHT

The weight is used to stabilize the basket whilst under construction. I use flat-bottomed stones of various sizes. Anything that is small and dense

Opposite: The basic tool set. (Top to bottom:) grease horn; bodkins; secateurs; hand knives; rapping iron; weight; sharpening stone. (At right:) screwblock.

enough to stop the basket from tipping is suitable, e.g. a flat iron.

GREASE HORN

Traditionally, this was a tallow-filled horn but today (more realistically) it is likely to be any sort of unbreakable container filled with some sort of lubricant and used to ensure that the bodkin is always sufficiently greased to ease it through the weave. Tallow (sheep's fat) can be a bit tricky to get hold of these days although chicken factories sometimes use it to strip the feathers off the birds. Lanolin, lard or soap can be used as good substitutes. Melt the tallow, or its substitute, and mix it with either plumber's hemp, wire wool, woodshavings or similar, and let it set around your bodkin in the container.

MISCELLANEOUS ESSENTIALS

In addition to this basic set of tools you will also need an old sack, curtain or blanket for 'mellowing' and a ruler or tape-measure. A plant spray to keep the rods damp when working and a hoop made from willow or string to keep the stakes upright. Keep a few clothes-pegs handy to hold sections of weave temporarily in place and a sharpening stone to keep your tools ready for use.

SPECIALIZED TOOLS

The cleave, shave and upright are specialized tools most commonly used when producing very fine baskets and materials for chair-seating.

Specialized tools.

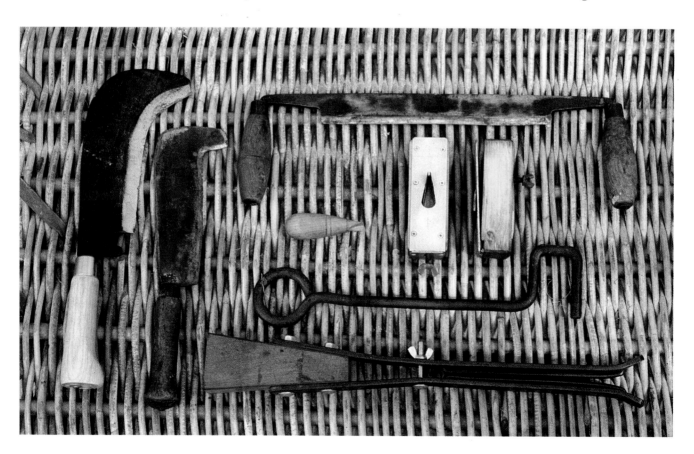

BRAKE

This is a device used for stripping the bark off willow to make white rods. Each rod is pulled through two flexible metal shafts. You would only be likely to need it if you have grown your own willow. Machinery is now used to do this job on commercial willow farms.

CLEAVE

A cleave is an egg-shaped device with three or four points at one end. It is used for splitting dry rods prior to skeining.

SHAVE

This is used for removing the pith from willow skeins.

UPRIGHT

This is used to even the width of willow skeins.

COMMANDER

A commander is a sturdy metal bar used to iron out kinks in rods. It is only really used when using longer, thicker rods to make bigger baskets. For most purposes, just be sure to select the straightest rods for the upright sticks and the wiggly ones for the side weaving.

BILLHOOK

A billhook is a heavy slashing tool traditionally used for harvesting the willow crop

DRAWKNIFE

A drawknife is a traditional green-woodworking blade used for shaping wood and stripping off bark

THE WORKSHOP

Without doubt, the most important aspect of any basketry workshop is that it should have plenty of floor and ceiling space. Whether the baskets are made on the floor, on a table or on a lapboard, even the smallest basket in progress is going to take up a lot of space. It would be easy to take an eye out with a flicking willow rod as you weave, so your work should be kept well clear of other people. If working outside, ensure that your soaked willow rods do not dry out in the hot summer sun by spraying water on them with a garden sprayer.

I generally make my baskets on a table, but other basketmakers may find themselves a kindly cushion and sit on the floor to make them. Some basketmakers use a lapboard, which is a piece of hard-board or similar, with one end resting comfortably between your knees and the other on the floor. A cross of holes is drilled at the lap end so that the basket can be pinned in place by the bodkin and revolved around as it is being worked. Whichever method is used, it should be the one that is the most physically comfortable choice.

Basketmaking tends to be a dirtier and messier job than most people would expect it to be. As you work, the trimmings from the baskets tend to fly off in all directions and get lodged in every nook and cranny in the workshop. An easy-to-sweep workshop is helpful, for obvious reasons. One other aspect that is important to remember, when you and your new-found enthusiasm have eventually been exiled from the house to the potting shed, is warmth. Basketmaking can sometimes be a very sedentary activity, so a heated workshop is also an advantage, making the whole experience more pleasurable.

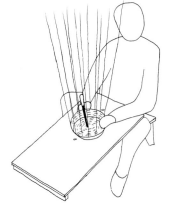

Using the lapboard.

INTRODUCTORY TECHNIQUES

The remaining chapters explain some of the techniques used in stake and strand, and frame basketry. These types of basketry techniques are the ones most commonly associated with the British tradition of basketmaking today. They are also the most commonly used techniques in British hedgerow work. Beginning with these methods is a good basis upon which to take your interest further, should you wish to try some other ways of making baskets later. These chapters on basic techniques, together with the projects at the end of the book, are designed to be used in conjunction with each other when making your first few baskets. They are written with a scale of difficulty in mind, so that the first of the projects will also relate directly to the early chapters on basic techniques. The fact that the chapter on framework is at the end, does not imply that making frame baskets is more difficult than making stake and strand work – it isn't – but merely that making frame baskets involves the use of some methods, which are entirely different to those of stake and strand work. However, I do recommend that you attempt some round-stake and strandwork before approaching any framework. The round shape is by far the easiest to achieve and will enable you to become reasonably confident using some basic weaves, without also needing to concentrate too much on achieving the right shape. Once you have broken the back of some roundwork you can proceed to oval, square and framework.

The base sticks and uprights should always be made of much stouter sticks than the weavers, otherwise they will be outweighed as you work up the basket. Not only will this give the finished basket a very unbalanced appearance but it will also be very difficult to maintain the intended shape. As a general guide, rods of 3–4ft are more suitable for smaller, finer work, such as bread-baskets and trays; rods of 4–5ft are better for baskets, such as shoppers; rods of 5–8ft are good for log baskets and laundry baskets; and so on. The bigger the basket, the bigger the rods you will need. Don't be disappointed if the first few baskets turn out a bit wobbly, with a bit of perseverance the knack comes pretty quickly and you can always use your first baskets as a gauge to see how much you are improving! Maintain firm control over the uprights and weavers as you work up the basket – don't let them master you. By being determined and 'placing' each rod exactly where you want it to go before moving onto the next, the weaving will be easier and the standard of your work will progress much more quickly.

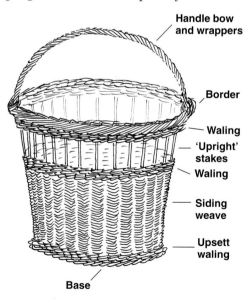

Anatomy of a stake and strand basket.

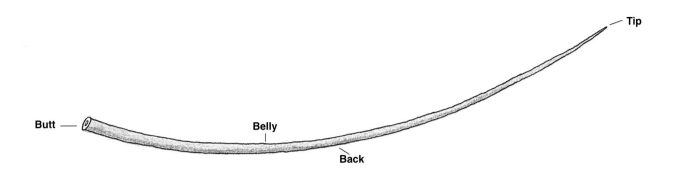

Butt

Belly

Back

Tip

Rod anatomy.

The definition of a round, oval or square basket is set by its base. A round-based basket may have an oval rim at the top, but it is still defined as a 'round' basket because it uses roundwork construction techniques. The term squarework can sometimes appear confusing because most squarework baskets are not actually square but rectangular or triangular, for instance. They are called 'square' because of their angled corners.

All rods, of whatever material, will have a belly and a back. Always work with the natural leaning of the rod and not against it. Facing the belly of the upright rods towards the inside will give you an outward bowing basket. Conversely, facing the belly of the upright rods towards the outside will give you a straight-sided basket. Pick rods that are as straight and even as you can for the uprights; any kinks or excessive bends will distort the shape of the basket.

NOTE FOR THE LEFT-HANDED READER

All the instructions in this book are written only with a right-handed person in mind. However, it is possible for the left-handed basketmaker to make use of the general instructions by reversing them or using a mirror.

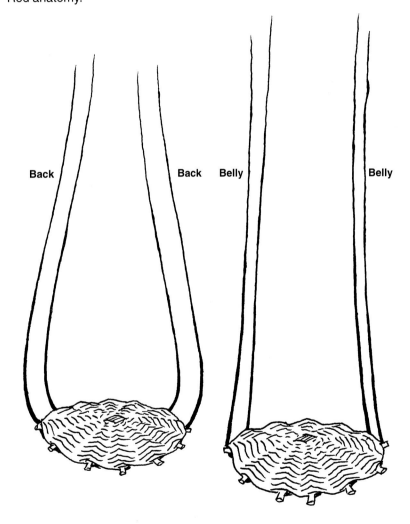

Back   Back   Belly   Belly

Staking-up using the bellies and backs of rods.

4 Bases

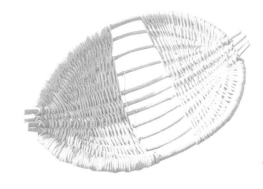

The base is one of the most important parts of a basket. It will define how the rest of the structure takes shape. It is worthwhile practising a few bases and trying to get them right before moving on to make the sides. An uneven or loosely woven base will make it difficult to weave the siding and will prevent the finished basket from sitting properly. The base stikes should be the stoutest in the whole basket and will determine the strength of the finished product.

The tendency at first is to make the base too large for the intended size of the finished basket, so think ahead quite carefully when making the base. Consider the desired circumference of the basket at the border, how much you want it to lean out and how many upright stakes will be needed for the siding. If there are too many bottom sticks, there will consequently be too many upright side stakes crowded together, and this will make the side-weaving difficult and tight. If there are too few base sticks there will be too few uprights and this will make the basket loose and wobbly. As a general rule, a larger base will require more base sticks than a smaller one.

It may be useful at first to observe other baskets around you to help gauge how many base sticks are needed for your basket. Bases are usually made with a slightly concave shape, so that the basket can sit on the rim of the base, giving it more stability and preventing it from bottoming out. This is particularly important if the basket is to hold a lot of weight.

ROUND BASES

Step 1. The first part of round-base construction involves making and tying in the slath. The slath is the cross-shaped arrangement of base sticks. To make the slath, cut six sticks from the butt ends of the stoutest rods you have collected for your basket. These will be the base sticks and should be slightly longer than the intended width of the base. Lay three together, so that the bellies and the backs all flow the same way. This will allow you to see the way the sticks should be tied in, to make a concave base. Make a split in the centre of the side of each stick by pushing and wiggling in the point of a handknife. Split the stick along the grain so that the gap is wide enough to fit the other three rods through. It should not be necessary to saw through the base sticks to make the gap.

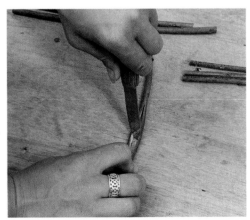

Splitting the slath sticks.

Step 2. *Slype* the ends of the three unsplit rods with a handknife to make it easier to pass these sticks through the splits you

Opposite: Bases.

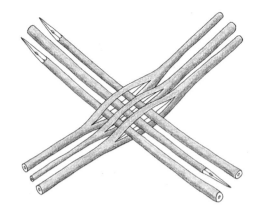

Threading the slath sticks.

THE SLYPE

A slype is a diagonal cut at the butt end of a rod. Strictly speaking it involves more than putting on a sloping cut with a pair of secateurs. It is most effectively achieved by trimming the rod with three or four strokes of a knife, so that an angled point is created. A good slype is essential in order to insert rods into tight places easily.

A slyped rod.

have made in the other three sticks. Pass these unsplit sticks, one at a time, through all three of the other split rods, ensuring that the thick and thin ends of all the sticks are alternately arranged, to help achieve a balanced base.

Step 3. At this point on the base the pairing begins. Pairing is the clockwise weave that will be used to make the whole base. Take two of the thinnest weaving rods of approximately equal length, trimming off the frayed ends if there are any. Holding the centre of the slath firmly in your left hand to keep the sets of sticks at right angles to one another, insert the tips of the weavers through the split on the left of a set of three base sticks. You should just be able to see the tips protruding through the other side of the split. Place the rods to the right, one laying in front and one behind the set of three base sticks. The ends of both pairing weavers should face the front.

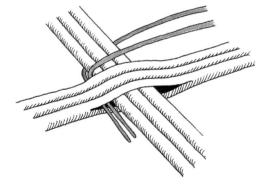

Threading the first pairing weavers through the slath.

Step 4. Take the left-hand weaver down to the back, away from you, and over the right-hand weaver, round the back of the next set of sticks and back out to the front again. Turn the slath 90 degrees and perform the same action with the other weaver. There should

Base pairing around the slath.

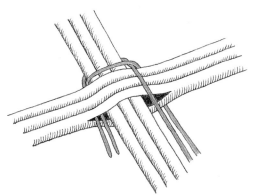

First pairing strokes around the slath.

still be one weaver in front and one weaver behind the base sticks, but they will have swapped places. Repeat these strokes until there are two rounds of pairing around the slath. It will look like as though a square has been tied around the centre.

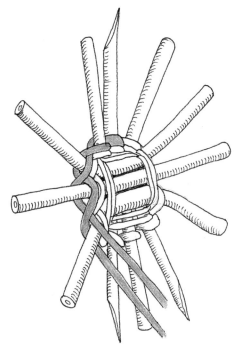

Side view of pairing on base.

Right: Randing join.
Below: Pairing join.

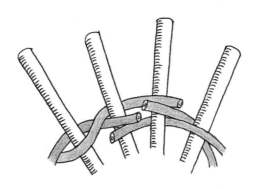

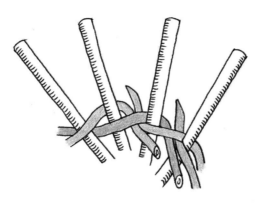

Step 5. The same pairing strokes are used to open out the base sticks. Leave

More than six base-sticks may be required to make larger round bases. In this instance, it may not be possible to open out all the base sticks on the first round of pairing, as the spaces may be too tight to weave through. Pair round and open them out into groups, e.g. into twos and threes before singling them out.

the centre base sticks at right angles to each other. Continue pairing in a clockwise direction, gradually easing out the base sticks as you do so. Try to pull the weavers as tightly and as close to the centre as possible, while aiming to make the base sticks equidistant. Don't worry if the base sticks are not equidistant after the first round, you can gradually work them into place with each round of weaving; but do try and get them into position as soon as possible. The aim is to lock the base sticks in place with the pairing weavers when they cross over each other. The concave shape is accentuated as necessary by the pairing as you weave around the base.

Step 6. When the butts of the first pair of weavers have been reached, you will have to join in a new pair in order to continue weaving by using a pairing join. Insert the second pair of weavers individually under and to the left of the used-up ends. This secures the old and new weavers in position. Alternatively, if you don't want any cut or butt ends

Opening out base sticks into groups.

showing on the top side of the base, just join in by leaving the ends of the previous weavers on the underside (this is called a 'randing join'). The randing join method may look more attractive but it won't be as strong. To create an even-looking base, always join in tips-to-tips and butts-to-butts.

Step 7. Continue to pair and join in around the base until the required size has been reached, using the finest weavers first. It is possible to gradually increase the size of the pairing rods as the radius gets bigger. You will quickly realize that it would be impossible to tie in the slath with anything but a very fine rod. Finish with tips so as not create an awkward step at the outer circumference. Tuck the tip ends into the previous round of weaving to prevent it from unravelling.

Step 8. Using the secateurs, trim off the ends of the base weavers flush against the weave of the base by make a sloping cut that will leave the cut end of the weaver lying neatly and securely against a base stick. Be careful not to cut it too short, so that it slips through to the other side. Trim the ends of the slath sticks as close to the edge of the base as possible.

OVAL BASES

Once you have got to grips with some round bases you can feel more confident about approaching the oval ones. The section on round bases illustrated how to do base pairing and control the slath whilst weaving. When you are familiar with these aspects of making a base you can concentrate on how to achieve the oval shape. Oval bases have a tendency to twist as they are woven. To counteract this tendency another weave called 'reverse pairing' is used alongside

ordinary pairing. The base sticks of an oval base also have a tendency to slip around until the slath is firmly tied in. When cutting the length of your base sticks consider what shape of oval you are trying to achieve – elongated or rotund. The final shape of the oval will be determined by the number of long and short base sticks, and also the distance from the end of the long sticks to the end of the short outer sticks.

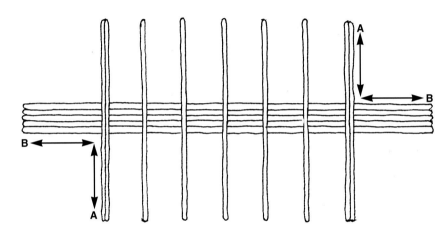

Step 1. Cut a set of stout base sticks. Depending on the size of base, you will need three to four long sticks and six to eight shorter sticks for an average-sized base and basket. Make splits in all the short sticks wide enough for all the long sticks to fit through. Slype one end of each of the long sticks to ease their passage through the splits. Thread the long sticks through the short sticks one at a time, ensuring that the thick and thin ends are alternated. You may find inserting these long sticks a little easier if you tap down the first long stick against one side of the split to make room for the others to pass. Remember to keep the bellies and backs flowing the same way.

Step 2. Space all the sticks out evenly leaving two sets of two at equal

A & B should be equal distances.

CHASING

Chasing is a frequently used technique, which involves weaving two or more sets of rods at once. It is done by weaving the first set of rods until you meet the beginning of the second set; dropping the first set and weaving with the second until you meet the first set again, and so on. Do not to let the sets of weavers overtake each other. In this way the weavers follow or 'chase' each other round.

REVERSE PAIRING

Putting on a round of reverse pairing does not mean that you can just turn the work over and work upside down! Rather it involves using a different stroke. Reverse pairing is indeed very similar to ordinary pairing, except that it is worked from the front to the back. Leave the ends of the pairing weavers on the underside, instead of the top, of the base as you work. Using ordinary and reverse pairing in conjunction gives an attractive chain effect to the weave. These combined strokes are described as 'chain pairing'. It is also possible to work rounds of reverse and ordinary pairing separately in blocks instead of simultaneously.

distances from the ends. The slath is tied in and the base sticks opened out by using two sets of pairing weavers. This technique of using two sets of weavers is called 'chasing'. In the case of an oval base, ordinary pairing and reverse pairing are chased around to counteract the twisting that can occur.

Step 3. Insert the tip ends into the splits of the double sticks on alternate sides. As in round-base construction, the slath should be paired round twice to secure it into position before beginning to open out the base sticks.

Step 4. As mentioned above, two different types of pairing chase each other round the base to counteract the twist. Take one set of weavers and pair round in the normal way until you reach the beginning of the second set. Keep the pairing as close to the slath as possible. The first row of pairing on oval

Effect of chain pairing.

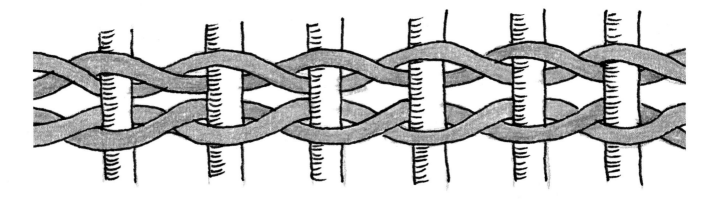

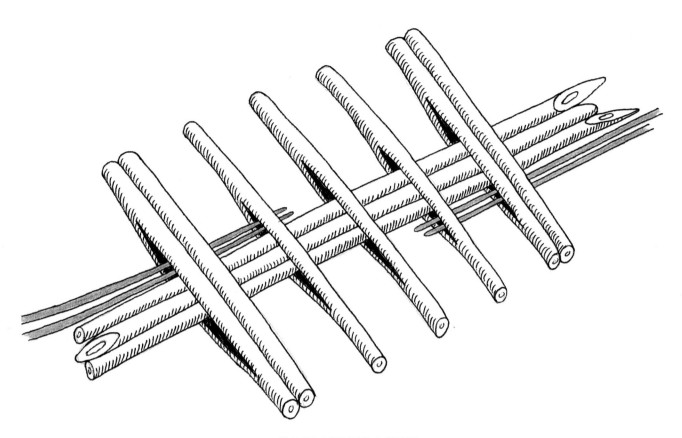

bases has a greater tendency to slip away from the slath until the second round has been put on – so be determined. The reverse pairing is begun with the second set of weavers.

Step 5. After putting on a couple of rounds of pairing to tie in the slath, start to open out the base sticks. Since the side sticks already lay in singles, it is not necessary to separate these but you do need to open out the end sticks into a fan shape. Join in with tips-to-tips and butts-to-butts on the long sides only. Joining in at the ends will make the base weak. Continue pairing and reverse pairing until the required size has been reached. Finish with tips and tuck them away into the previous row of pairing. Trim off the ends of the weavers and cut the ends of the base sticks off as close to the edge of the base as possible.

SQUARE BASES

A screwblock is used to help make the square base. Since squarework base sticks are not bent in order to form the shape there is no need to soak them. As you weave up the base be careful to keep the outer sticks parallel as they have a tendency to draw in, leaving a base that is narrower at one end than the other – this will detrimentally affect the shape of the finished basket and should be avoided. Unlike the round or oval bases, square bases should be kept as flat as possible, so take care that the inside sticks do not lean backwards or forwards.

Step 1. Cut a set of the stoutest butt ends 8–10cm longer than the intended base length from straight dry rods. The number of base sticks will vary with the

Pairing weavers inserted to start an oval base.

size of the basket. Take half of the base sticks and shave or slype the butt ends so that they are the same width as the tip ends. Insert the sticks at even intervals into the screwblock; thick and thin ends alternately arranged. Place two sticks together at the outer edges. Tighten the screwblock so that none of the sticks move about.

Step 2. Begin weaving the square base with a row of pairing. Select a rod more than double the length of the width of the base. Loop the rod around the bottom of the left-hand pair of sticks, making sure that the butt end will reach to the other side of the base when woven in. Pair with the two lengths you have created to the other side of the base.

Step 3. Leave the butt end resting against the outer sticks. Wrap the tip end twice around the right-hand pair of sticks and then begin randing with the remainder back towards the left-hand pair of sticks. As the left-hand pair of

Weaving the first rod on a square base.

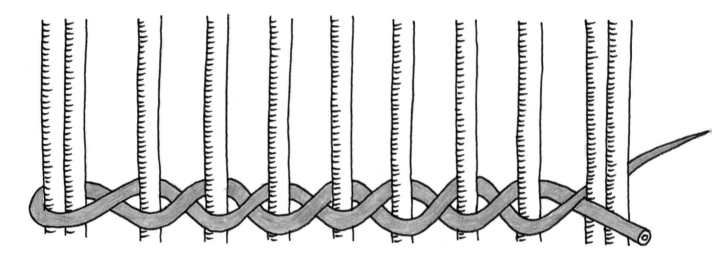

Randing stroke and join.

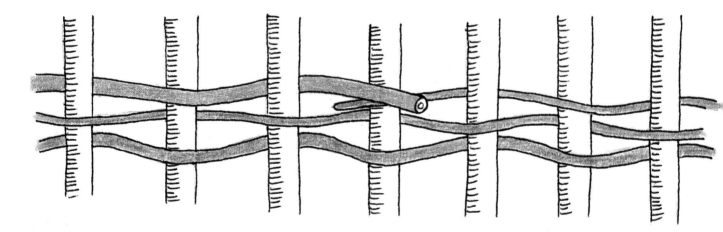

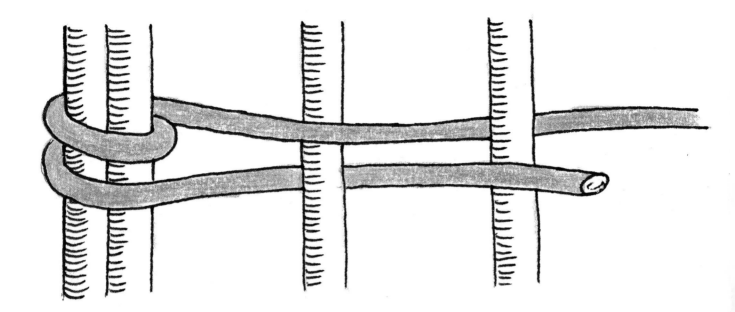

outer base sticks is reached again, wrap the weaver around them and begin randing back to the right. When the tip end runs out, join in with a butt, laying it on top of the tip and ensuring that the butt will be on the underside of the base. Always join in with a butt and never join in near the outer sticks, as this will make the base weak.

Step 4. Continue randing back and forth between the outer sticks all the way up the base, constantly checking that the outer sticks remain parallel, especially as you wrap around the outer sticks. (As a gauge to help you keep the outer sticks parallel, use a stick cut to the same width as the bottom of the base.) To keep the progress of the randing weave level, wrap the randing weaver round the outer sticks twice, at frequent intervals, before weaving back towards the other side. Use the rapping iron to gently tap down the weave every few rounds, this will help to keep the weave dense. Pay particular attention to rapping down the

outer edges but take care that it does not draw in the outer sticks.

Step 5. When the required height has been reached, simulate the pairing with the last weaver by weaving under and over the previous row. Take the base out of the screwblock and trim off the protruding ends of the weavers against the underside of the base sticks. Trim off the ends of the base sticks flush with the base.

Double-wrapping on outer sticks.

RANDING
Randing is a very easy weave and simply involves weaving in front of and behind the upright stakes.

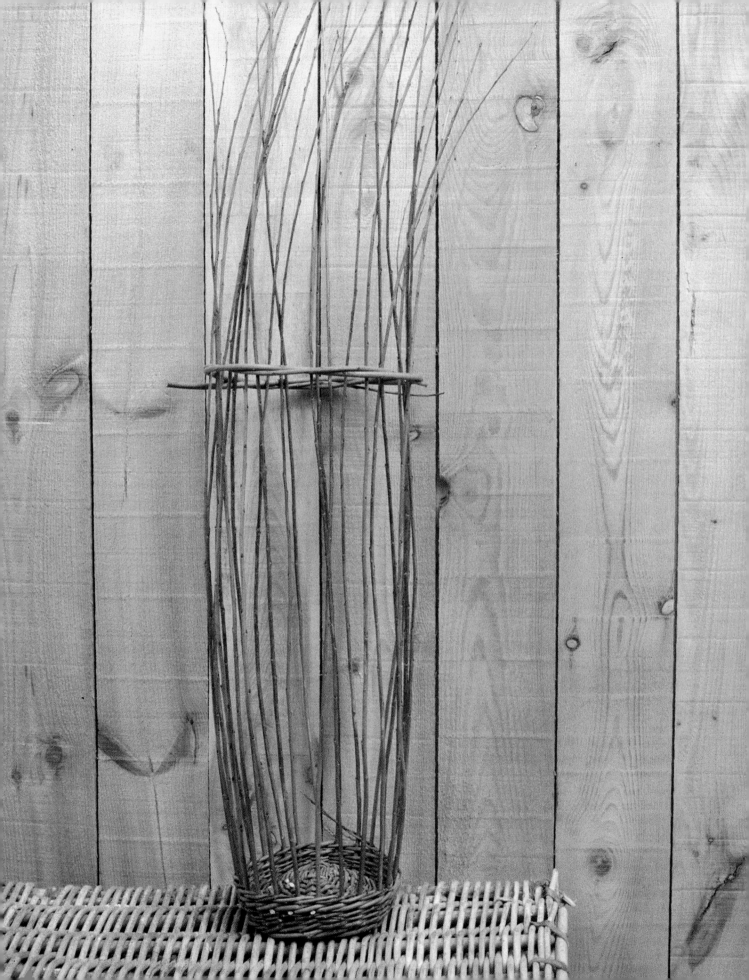

5 Staking-Up and the Upsett

Staking-up and putting on the upsett provides the main frame-work for all stake and strand baskets; and involves inserting a set of thick rods into the base, bending them up and tying them securely into position with a row of weavers. The upright rods should be carefully selected to ensure that they are as straight and even as possible, and should be thinner than the base sticks but thicker than the weavers. If you want the basket to bow outwards at the sides, slype the rods selected for the uprights on the back; if you want a straight-sided basket slype the rods on the belly (*see* page 29). When selecting rods for the uprights, consider how tall the basket will eventually be and how thick you want the border. The upright rods will also be used to lay down the border. Bending-up the uprights is called 'pricking-up'; the upsett is achieved by putting on two or three rows of a weave called 'waling'; and the whole process of putting in the uprights, pricking-up and putting on the upsett is called 'staking-up'.

STAKING-UP ROUND BASES

Step 1. In roundwork an upright stick is inserted into the weave on either side of each of the radial base-sticks. Select as many straight rods as you consequently need and slype the butt ends. If six base-sticks have been used, there will be

twelve radial sticks around the slath and you will need to put on twenty-four uprights. If eight base-sticks have been used there will be sixteen radial base-sticks around the slath and you will need to select thirty-two upright rods. The slype on the butt should be inserted into the base face down, so that it cannot be seen when the base is finished; you will need to remember this when slyping the bellies or backs of the upright rods and planning the intended curve on the finished basket.

Step 2. Using a well-greased bodkin, open a channel down one side of a base stick, and insert an upright rod as far as it will go into the base. The further the rod is pushed in the more secure it will be. Continue inserting a slyped rod on either side of all the base sticks. If the base is large it may be easier to do this by holding the upturned base underfoot.

Step 3. You will now need to prick-up the uprights. Place the base with its underside down, resting on its rim.

Rods inserted into a round base underfoot.

Opposite: Staked-up basket with upsett woven on.

Kinking the rods with a knife.

WALING WEAVE

Waling is a very strong weave woven clockwise, and is put on all stake and strand baskets at strategic points where extra strength is needed. It can also be used to help change the flow or shape of a basket or to outline the texture of various weaves; but it is always used to put on the upsett. The waling on the upsett is usually started by using four-rod waling at first; then one rod is dropped and three-rod waling is used to continue the weave. Two sets of waling weavers are put on, on opposite sides of the basket and chased around. On very small baskets it is possible just to use one set.

Gently press the tip of a handknife along the grain of the inserted rod, as close to the rim of the base as possible. As you press, lightly twist the knife and bend the rod upwards: the aim is to kink the rod upright at 90 degrees without snapping it in the process. Twisting the knife, as you bend up the rod, splits open the grain and renders the rod more pliable. Once the rod has been successfully kinked, let it drop and proceed to do the same with the rest of the rods. Place a weight on top of the base and gather all the kinked rods up, placing a hoop or a piece of string around them to keep them upright. Collecting the rods up is easier if you gradually gather them in from opposite sides of the base. Ensure the rods are evenly spaced and are not tangled up at the top.

You will now have to put the upsett on the basket. The function of the upsett is to attach the uprights firmly to the

Three-rod waling.

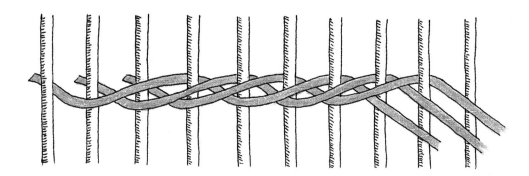

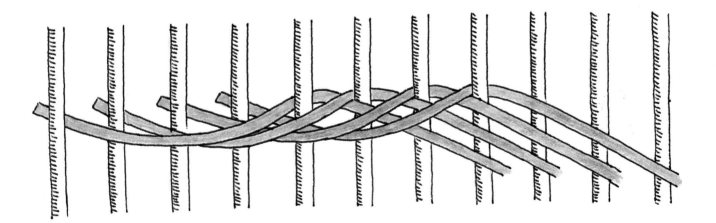

base and, also, to evenly space the rods out prior to the main weaving. The upsett, put on with a 'waling' weave, is also an important device for helping to determine the future shape of the basket.

Step 4. Select eight medium-width rods (thinner than the upright stakes), each long enough to go right around the basket. Trim off any frayed tips and slype the butts on the belly. Insert four slyped rods as far as you can to the left of the previously inserted uprights. This will be a tight squeeze but is again made easier by making a channel with a greased bodkin first. Insert the other four rods in the same way on the opposite side of the base.

Step 5. To begin the four-rod waling,

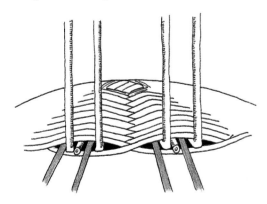

Inserted waling rods.

take the left-hand rod and pass it to the right in front of three upright stakes, behind the next upright and back out to the front again. The first waling rod should go over the top of the other three waling weavers. Complete the same strokes with the remaining waling weavers until you have gone half-way around the base. Pull the waling weavers firmly down against the edge of the base as you complete each stroke. This creates a sturdy rim on the base and helps to avoid leaving large gaps in the basket between the base and the siding. Putting on the first round of waling may be easier if you hold the basket between the knees or, if working on a table, pull it to the edge.

Step 6. Continue by chasing the waling, i.e. having woven the first set of weavers half-way around the basket, begin waling with the second set of weavers until you reach the beginning of the first again. At this point on the upsett, the foremost waling weaver is dropped. Waling continues with three rods on each side of the basket.

Proceed with the three-rod wale by passing the left-hand weaver over two stakes to the right, round the back of the next upright and to the front again. Weaving a three-rod wale is almost

Four-rod waling.

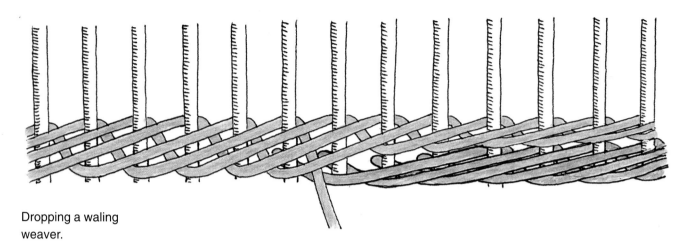

Dropping a waling weaver.

exactly the same as weaving a four-rod wale, except for the fact that you pass over one less upright stake. Continue chasing with a three-rod wale round the basket until you reach the tips. Tap the weave down with a rapping iron.

Step 7. When the rods run out, new ones are joined in by inserting a new set of three weavers alongside the tips. (It helps if you imagine that you are extending the length of the weaver that has run out.) Join in tips-to-tips and butts-to-butts, and continue waling until about three or four rounds have been put on the upsett. If you wish you can put on more rounds of waling for decorative purposes. By the finish of the upsett, all the upright stakes should be evenly spaced. No individual stake should be obviously leaning in or out of the basket.

STAKING-UP OVAL BASES

Putting the upsett on an oval base differs to round base upsetts. Only the long end sticks have two uprights inserted on either side of them. The short side-sticks have only one upright inserted beside them, otherwise the gaps between the uprights would be too crowded. Prick-up the side stakes and put on the upsett (*see* pages 41–4), starting the wale on the straight sides not the rounded ends. Once the uprights have been pricked-up, keep them upright in an oval hoop.

Joining in new waling weavers.

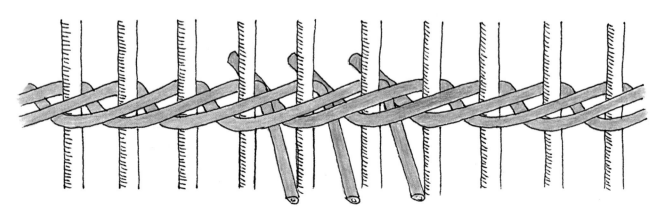

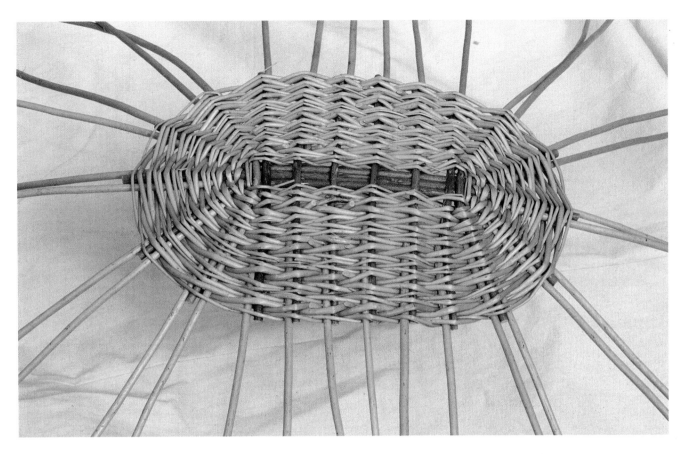

STAKING-UP SQUARE BASES

Some of the techniques involved in squarework are quite advanced and it may take a good deal of practice before you can guarantee achieving the desired shape. Care needs to be taken when putting the upsett on a square base. Just as the oval base can twist when putting on the pairing, so the square base can twist when putting on the upsett. Stakes for squarework should be slyped on the belly so that when they are inserted and pricked up, the line of the rod is vertical, not bowed outwards. The corners on a square basket are made by inserting two stakes at right angles to each other at the corners of the base and keeping them as close and parallel to each other as possible when weaving up the sides.

Step 1. Calculate how many uprights are needed. Two rods will be needed for each corner and the remainder should be positioned so that they are evenly spaced after the upsett has been put on. Mark the position of the uprights for the sides with a pencil.

Step 2. Insert the uprights into the ends of the base first, slyping them on the belly and inserting them into the weave at least a couple of inches. Make a channel with a greased bodkin if necessary. Usually only one upright per end stick needs to be inserted but the centre end-sticks may need an upright inserted on either side of them in order to create an even spacing of uprights after the upsett has been put on. Position the rest on whichever side will create an even spacing. Always insert an upright

Inserted stakes in an oval base.

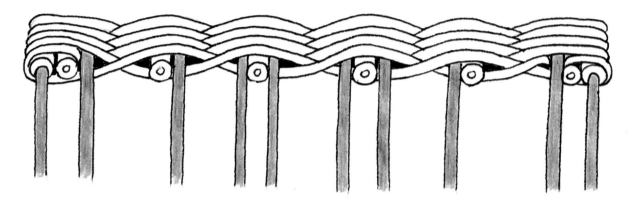

Position of uprights on end of a square base.

in the gaps right next to the outer sticks. When pricked and woven up this collection of uprights will help to define the shape of the corner. Prick-up and tie-up the rods with a hoop.

Step 3. With a greased bodkin, force a hole in the pith of the outer end-sticks and push a slyped butt in each as far as it will go. With a handknife, put a kink in these rods beyond the slype and tap them in up to the elbows and the edge of the outer sticks using the rapping iron. The rods must be kinked beyond the slype, otherwise they will split. These rods will act as one-half of the corner uprights. Bend the rods up and put them into the hoop along with the other uprights.

Step 4. A greased bodkin is needed to help you insert all the uprights into the sides. First put in the other half of the corner sticks. Starting as close to the corners as you can, pierce the two outer sticks on all four corners diagonally towards the centre of the basket. Insert slyped rods into the split, slype down, kink them and tap them in with the rapping iron, so that they re-emerge between the weave on the inside of the basket. You should now have all eight corner stakes in place.

Step 5. Pierce slightly upwards through the two outer sticks to make a gap for the

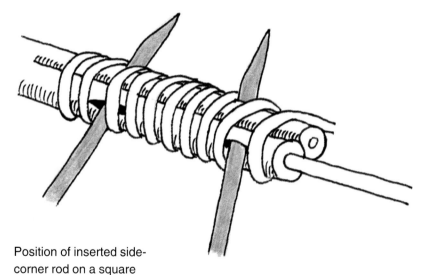

Position of inserted side-corner rod on a square base.

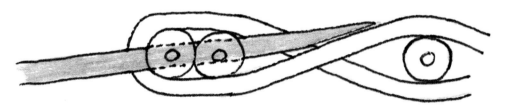

Angle of inserted side stake on a square base.

remainder of the upright rods at the places you have marked with the pencil. Insert the remaining upright rods into the gaps. Prick-up these rods and keep upright with the hoop. You may need to use two hoops to hold all the uprights in position on squarework. Trim the end sticks so that they are flush with the edge of the base.

Step 6. Putting the upsett on a square base is very similar to putting it on round and oval bases. Select eight medium-sized weavers, so that two sets of four-rod waling can be chased around the basket. Gather together four trimmed tips and hook them round the bottom of an upright stake in the middle of the long side of the basket. Gradually work out the tips to their four-rod waling position. Do the same with the other set of four rods on the opposite side of the basket and begin chasing the waling round until the butts are reached. Drop one waler and join in with another three butts to continue with each set of waling until you reach the tips again.

When first approaching the ends of the base with the waling, take care to pull down the weaving rods as far as you can in order to conceal as much of the ends as possible. Try to keep the corner uprights parallel to one another. Avoid joining in the waling near the corners, as this will weaken the basket and make it difficult to achieve an even weave at the corners.

BYE STAKES

Bye stakes are extra stakes inserted next to the existing uprights after the upsett has been put on. They are used to give extra strength and width to the uprights, if the weavers are rather thick. This can be extremely useful in hedgerow work when it is sometimes difficult to find very fine weavers. Bye stakes are also frequently used on baskets that are fitched. They reduce the distance between the original upright stakes and thereby enable a stronger and neater fitch.

Bye stakes are put in by selecting the same number of additional rods or thick sticks as the uprights you already have. Cut these extra sticks to approximately the height of the intended basket, or slightly higher (they can be trimmed off later). Slype and insert the thin ends in the gap in the weave to the left or right of the original upright. Inserting the thin end first ensures an even width of stake all the way up the side of the basket. Weave round both sticks as though they were one, if using them for extra strength. Separate them out on the next row of waling, if using them for fitched work. When the siding of the basket has been completed, trim off the tops of the bye stakes flush with the top row of waling and put the border down as usual. Bye stakes can also be used to make a double-rod border by inserting whole rods instead of short sticks (*see* Chapter 8).

Above: Bye stakes.

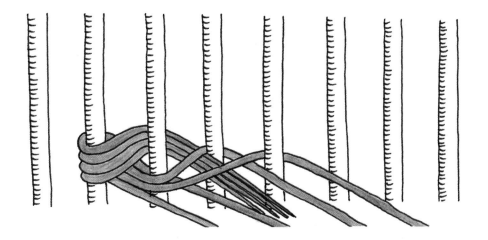

Laying weavers out into four-rod waling position.

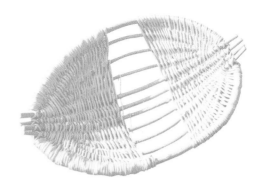

6 Weaves

The following weaves are usually used in the siding of baskets, which is where the basket really begins to take shape. There is a huge variety of weaves you can use for the siding, especially if you draw on influences from other parts of the world, but it is a good idea to get really familiar with some traditional ones first.

Waling, which has already been illustrated in Chapter 6, is always used at least twice on a basket: at the top and bottom. It can also be used to separate the panels of weaving on the sides and for reigning in the stakes if you feel you are loosing control of the shape of the basket. It is also possible to use waling for the whole of the siding of a basket to great decorative effect. This use of waling is particularly useful when making hedgerow-work, since the broad stroke of the waling weave allows the use of material that would otherwise not be pliable enough for side weaving.

Pairing, which has also already been illustrated in Chapter 6, is rarely used for siding – partly because there are so many other more attractive weaves to use. It is not particularly strong when put on this part of the basket and it is difficult to control the flow of the shape. There is no reason why you shouldn't experiment with pairing, however. (For pairing and waling weaves, *see* Chapter 6.)

ENGLISH RANDING

Randing is the simplest of all weaves and just involves weaving in and out of the uprights with one rod at a time. English randing is worked in a clockwise direction and uses up a whole rod at once before moving on to the next.

Opposite: English rand in progress.

Random woven nest by Lizzie Farey.

TIP

Once you are familiar with some of the basic weaves, you could even begin to make up your own. Some contemporary artist basketmakers use a technique called 'random weaving', which, as it sounds, is not really a rigidly structured weave at all but a series of random strokes that give a tangled nest-like effect. Deciding which is the most important facet of your planned basket (e.g. size, strength, colour, texture, aroma or utility), will help determine which materials and weaves are most suitable. If you wish to emphasize the colour of the material you have, it may be best to choose a smoother, cleaner weave for the siding. If you are using a weak hedgerow material, use plenty of waling to give the basket a strength that the material itself lacks. Experiment and see what effects can be achieved by using different combinations of weaves, textures and colours.

TIP
Remember it is the weaver that should bend for the upright and not the other way around. Hold the upright between the thumb and forefinger of your left hand, while weaving with the right, as you work around the basket. This will help to control the position of the stakes.

Finger and thumb positions for weaving.

Step 1. Select as many rods as there are uprights. They should be slightly thinner than the uprights and long enough to reach around the circumference of the basket, once their ragged tips and butts have been trimmed off.

Step 2. Place the butt of the first rod facing the inside of the basket and resting against the back of an upright. Take the rod in front of the next stake on the right and weave it behind the stake after that, in front of the next stake and so on. Continue weaving in and out of the stakes right around the basket until you have reached the butt of the first weaver again. Don't let the tip overlap the butt.

Step 3. Take the second weaver and place the butt one place to the right of the butt of the previous weaver. Weave in and out as described in the previous step, until you have once again reached the butt. The tip of the second weaver should pass over the butt and the tip of the first weaver, but not over its own butt. Continue like this until all the weaving rods have been used up.

You will notice, as the siding is worked up, that one side of the weaving is higher than the other. This is quite normal in English randing and is the result of using material with a natural taper. The level of the work will gradually even out as more weavers are put on. Rap the work down at frequent intervals.

Step 4. English randing has a spiral effect when it is completed. This can be decoratively emphasized by first passing each rod in front of two uprights before proceeding with the weave as normal.

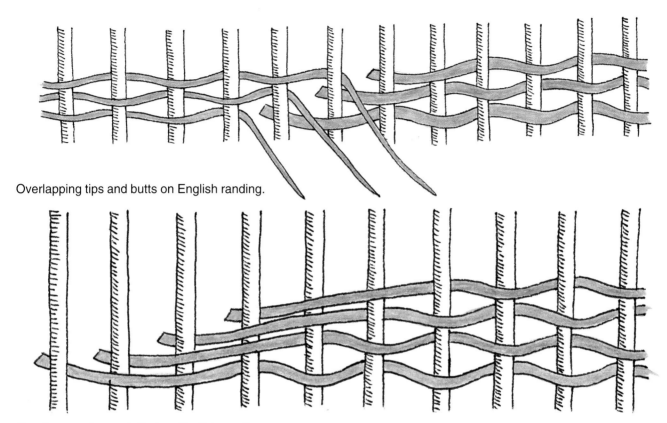

Overlapping tips and butts on English randing.

Passing over two rods first on English randing.

SLEWING

Slewing is useful for using up the tip ends that have been cut off another finished basket. It is a good weave to use if the uprights are a different colour to the weavers, creating an effective contrast. The weavers for slewing must be much finer than the uprights, as several weavers will be randed in parallel in a single stroke; if the weavers are not fine, it will put a distorting strain on the uprights. The more slewing weavers you use, the thicker the uprights need to be; either that or use finer weavers. It is possible to slew with anything from two to six rods at once. If there are an odd number of uprights on the basket, put on a single, continuous row of slewing. If there are an even

Slewed log basket.

number of stakes, two sets of slewing will have to be chased. Slewing is always laid in butt ends first.

Step 1. Select a quantity of weavers for the slew. The number of weavers required depends on the width of the panel of weaving and the size of the basket, and not the number of uprights. You will just have to estimate how many fine weavers

the weavers on the outside or continue with one set on an odd number of uprights.

Step 3. If chasing the slewers, start randing with another single rod by placing the first butt of the second set of weavers behind the stake that the previously used set of slewing weavers are in front of. There should be a set of

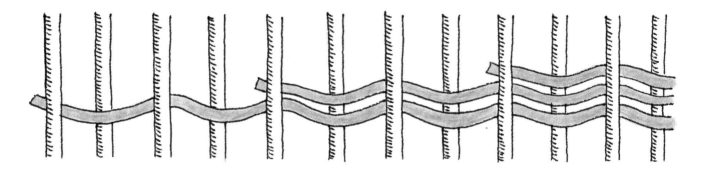

Starting and adding in on the slew.

will be needed to complete the sides. This will become easier to gauge when you have made one or two slewed baskets.

Step 2. Starting with a single butt placed behind an upright, rand a weaver half-way along its length. Add in another weaver butt-end first, above and parallel to the first, and rand them together until you are half-way along the length of the second weaver. Add in another weaver in the same way, if necessary. If there is an even number of uprights, you will have to continue by 'chasing' another set of slewing weavers. Leave the tip ends of

weavers behind a stake and a set of weavers in front of a stake as you chase round the basket. Gradually add in another couple of weavers, as described above. You should now have two sets of slewing rods that are beginning to chase each other around the basket.

Step 4. When either chasing a slew or using a single set, add in another slewing rod each time a weaver at the bottom of the group reaches its tip and runs out. In this way the slewing is kept continuous and of equal width until the desired height has been reached. At no

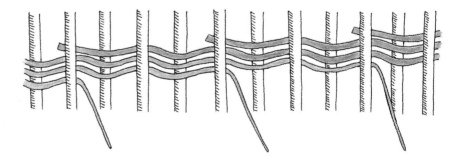

Adding butts and dropping tips.

time should two rounds or sets of slewing weavers go behind or in front of a single stake together. If they do when you are using chasing, you have probably made a mistake at the beginning of the first set; perhaps by inserting the first butt of the second set behind the wrong upright.

Step 5. If you plan to use a wide slew with a lot of weavers, you will probably need to add in new butts before reaching the half-way point of the rods below. This will ensure that the required number of rods is being slewed before finishing the first round.

FRENCH RANDING

French randing is different to English randing in that all the rods are woven simultaneously instead of one at a time, which makes it a little bit more complicated. It is also worked in an anticlockwise direction. The prospect of working the French rand can seem a little daunting at the start when all the weavers are first in position. Just remember it looks more difficult than it actually is. There is no spiral effect on the weave itself, unlike the English rand, but it can be used to make spirals if blocks of colour are used.

Step 1. Select the same number of weavers as upright stakes. Trim them so that they are the same length. Laying the butts in first, place the rods in as you would for the first stroke of an English rand, i.e. rest the butt behind an upright stake, take it over the front of the next rod to the right, behind the next stake and out to the front again. All the rods

French randing in progress.

Method of laying in
French randing weavers.

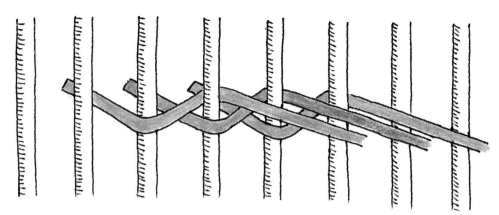

are put on the basket in this way before the weaving begins but they are put in one space to the left each time, instead of one space to the right as in English randing.

Step 2. The aim is to have a weaver emerging from every space between the stakes after they have all been laid in. Laying in the last couple of rods at the start of the French rand can be confusing at first, because it seems that there is nowhere to put them! When you have only two rods left to put in, lift the butts of the first two rods that you put in slightly upwards along the upright and insert the butts of the last two rods underneath them. Weave them in as you have done for the rest of the rods. Don't let the last two weavers cross over the first.

Step 3. To proceed with the weave, select any weaver and rand it one place to the right, leaving it on the outside of the basket. Do the same with the next weaver to the left and continue in this way with all the other weavers. You will notice when starting to weave the French rand that the first two weavers double up onto the next weavers to the right. This is what they are supposed to do. A pair of double weavers will continue to appear and travel right around the circumference of the basket until the panel of weaving has been finished.

Step 4. When the finish of the first round is approached you will have to deal appropriately with the double set of weavers before continuing. Use the bottom rod of each pair first, as these are

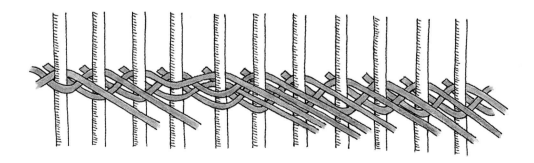

Beginning of French rand and the double weavers.

the ones that have not yet been randed. The top rods have already been randed at the start of the round of weaving. Continuing the weaving doubles up the weavers again.

Step 5. Continue randing like this until either the desired height has been reached or you have reached the tips. Single out the doubles on the last strokes of the last round, so that once again there is a rod emerging from every space. Try to estimate roughly

colours. Using butts first, rand to the right in front of two and behind two, bringing the rod out to the front again. Place the second and subsequent rods in two spaces to the left of the first and rand in the same way.

Step 2. Working in an anticlockwise direction, continue to rand in front of two and behind two with all the rods until you reach the tips. A narrow band of block weave will have been made. Rap the weaving down hard, getting rid

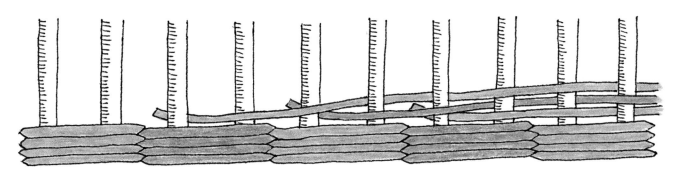

how long the weavers should be for the desired height before starting the weave. It makes for a neater finish if you actually finish the randing at the tips instead of cutting them off halfway along the rod.

BLOCK WEAVE

Block weave is an extremely attractive method of randing, especially if used with two or three different colours. Each round is rapped down very tightly so that no gaps are seen. This maximizes the effect of contrasting colours. No rounds of waling are put on between the rounds. Block weave can only be effectively used on round or oval work, since the angles on squarework are too steep for tight use of the blocks.
Step 1. Choose half as many weavers as there are stakes, preferably of alternate

of as much of the gap between the strokes as you can. Be careful that the weavers do not draw in the uprights and keep the uprights parallel.

Step 3. Weave the second and subsequent rounds one place to the right or left of the last round until the desired height has been reached.

FITCHING

Fitching allows large skeletal gaps to be left in the siding of the basket. It can be used to great decorative effect but is also extremely useful if you want to make a basket with good aeration, such as a cooling rack or an onion store. When the fitching weave has been put on the basket it looks like a row of reverse pairing but it is, in fact, worked quite differently. Don't make the

Block weave method.

Fitched basket by Trevor Leat.

Looping the tips round a stake.

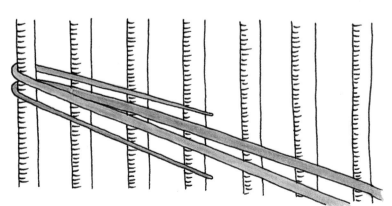

mistake of trying to put on a row of reverse pairing instead of fitching, as the pairing weave will look saggier and will probably eventually slip down the stakes into the gap left underneath. In order to put on a tight fitch, more stakes are needed than the normal proportion in stake and strand work. Usually this involves adding in bye stakes into the waling at the upsett. After finishing the waling upsett, make sure the tip ends are tucked well away, as there will be no further solid weave on top to fasten it in.

Step 1. Mark the height of the fitch on the basket with a pencil and select two very fine weavers. Loop the tips ends of the two weavers around a stake at fitching height. When weaving begins, use the tip ends of the weavers along with the rest of the rod so that they are secured in.

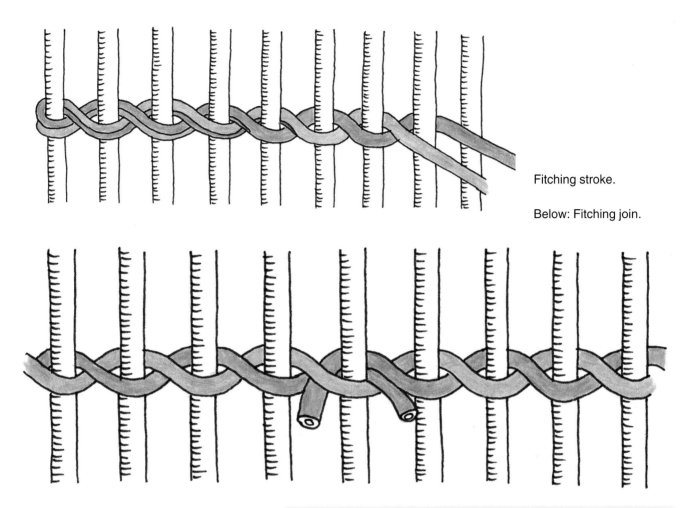

Fitching stroke.

Below: Fitching join.

Step 2. The theory is that the left-hand weaver (the one in front of a stake) passes over the underneath the right-hand weaver and behind the next stake to the right and out to the front again. The same action is completed with the weaver that was on the right but is now on the left. In practice, a tighter fitch is achieved if the two weavers are crossed over in one stroke, using both hands at once. Try to create as tight a twist as possible, giving the weavers two twists in between the stakes if the gap is large. Be consistent round the basket when deciding whether to use two twists or one, otherwise the fitching will look untidy.

PACKING

Packing is used where one area or side of a basket needs to be higher than another. It is usually put on with a straightforward randing weave and is very common on display baskets but can also be used on shopping or garden baskets, where the handle section of siding needs to be raised. Calculate (if helpful, mark with a pencil) where the centre and outer extremity of the packing is likely to lie, i.e. where your low points and high points are to be. Always using the butt of a weaver, packing can be started at the centre or the sides. Simply rand back and forth increasing or decreasing the number of uprights that are wrapped on each row. If more than one row of packing is needed to reach the desired height, start the packing in the centre and not the sides. This will give the total area of packing a neater finish.

Right: Packing from the sides.

Garden basket by Graham Glanville showing packing from centre and sides.

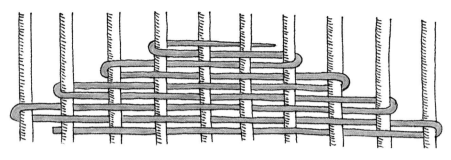

ALTERNATIVE START TO A PANEL OF WEAVING

An alternative start on a panel of weaving is a method that conceals the butt ends of the rods. This is useful when making items such as laundry baskets, where ends on the inside would catch on the cloth, and on screens, where trimmed butt ends would detract from the appeal of the design. Instead of laying the butt end on the inside behind and upright to start, slype the butt end and insert it into the weave to the right of an upright before continuing as normal.

Step 3. When the butts of the fitching weavers are reached, join in new butts, ensuring that the two joins are on separate areas of the circumference, otherwise the fitch will be weak. Be firm with the uprights while fitching, as they tend to slip out of position easily at first until you get the knack. When the start of the fitch has been reached again, pair round on top of the fitch until the tips run out. Tuck the tips away securely.

Far right: Cramming butt start.

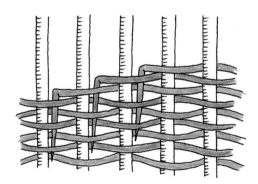

TIP

If you are caught out by a renegade rod that snaps while in the process of weaving (perhaps a piece made fragile by a patch of rust), don't panic! Join in and continue with the remainder of the rod as though you were using a new rod or select another that is of equal length and width from your pile of rods. Working with sections of rusted rod can be avoided by checking through the bundle before starting to weave.

7 Borders

Borders tie in the top to the bottom of the basket by making a decorative rim with the remaining length of the uprights. When deciding which type of border to use, consider its practicality as well as its attractiveness. For instance, if the basket is going to have a lid, it might be wise to lay down a narrow border, such as a trac border, so that it does not interfere with the fit of the lid. Also, a very wide border may not be appropriate for baskets that are to have handles, since it may be difficult to make their attachment look neat.

TRAC BORDERS

A simple trac border can look very attractive. Since it is a very narrow border it can be useful when making lidded baskets, although trac borders are used on other types of baskets too; sometimes being used for the whole siding of a basket. Trac borders are commonly associated with smaller baskets where strength is not necessarily of the essence. Its narrowness makes it a little weaker than some other types of border.

Step 1. Gently kink and release all the uprights around the top of the basket at a level that is at least slightly higher than the width of the uprights (i.e. high enough to allow the passage of uprights when they are bent down and weaved underneath the kink). You can place the kink up higher for a more decorative border but this is the minimum.

Step 2. To lay down a basic trac border, select any kinked upright, bend it down and pass it behind the next rod to the right, then in front of the next, leaving the tip pointing towards the inside of the basket. Repeat this stroke right around the basket. When the last upright at the end of the border is reached, continue the weave in the same way, making sure that it passes over the top of the previously worked rod but underneath the kink of the first rod. Trim off the basket with a sharp pair of secateurs.

The start of a behind one in front of one trac border.

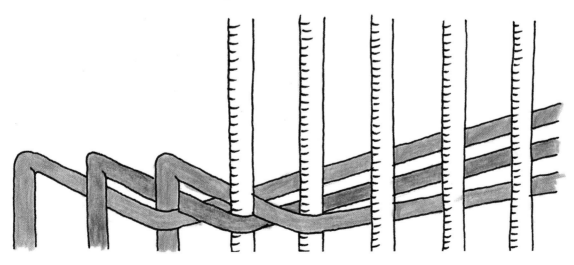

59

Step 3. As the border is worked, keep a regular pattern by ensuring that the uprights are consistently straight or sloping below the kink. Keep the horizontal level straight.

Varying the Trac Border

It is possible to vary the appearance of a trac border by altering its working only slightly, for example, by keeping the uprights straight or sloping, or bending, not kinking, the horizontal level of the uprights. This gives the border a gently rolling appearance instead of a hard edge. Try inserting another thin rod to the left of each upright and then bending the two down together. Vary the trac also by passing the rods in front of or behind two uprights instead of one, for example. However you put on the trac border, ensure consistent strokes.

Trimming Off the Basket

After the border has been finished, the tip ends of the uprights and any other weaving ends on the siding are trimmed off to finish the basket. They should be trimmed as close to the face of the basket as possible. Pull the border stakes and weavers slightly away from the basket and give them a sloping cut with the secateurs, so that the remaining section rests neatly against a stake and cannot slip through.

ROD BORDERS

Rod borders are much thicker and stronger than trac borders and are, therefore, much more hardwearing. They are used ubiquitously on both small and large baskets and can vary considerably

The finish of a behind one in front of one trac border.

FINISHING BORDERS

Finishing the border, i.e. where the beginning and the end of the border round meet, usually causes the most problems at first. Don't pull the first rods you bend down too tightly against the side of the basket, as this will make it difficult to weave the last border stakes. When finishing the border, it helps to try and imagine what you would do with the last remaining uprights, if the first uprights you bent down were still standing. The finishing strokes are exactly the same as they have been for the rest of the border, even though they make look different to begin with.

Avoid kinking the rod when finishing a border. Using the tips of the rods take as wide a bow as possible when threading the last rods through. If it helps, put a twist on the small section of the finishing border rod that rests behind the uprights on the inside of basket, before threading it back through to the outside. Make the rod more supple when finishing the border by firmly running the rod between the finger and thumb to break the grain up a little prior to threading it through.

Opposite: Five rods behind two border.

in size and thickness, depending on whether three to seven rods are used to lay it down. The less rods that are used, the narrower the border. The principle of laying a rod border down remains the same regardless of how many rods are used, however. The name of the rod border is determined by how many rods are bent down to start it.

Three Rods Behind One Border

Step 1. Kink and release three rods at the same height above the weaving. Leave enough room under the first kinks for the width of the finishing rods to pass through. Taking the first kinked rod on the left, bend it down behind the next rod to the right and out to the front again. Do the same with the next two kinked-down rods.

Bending down the first three rods on a three-rod border.

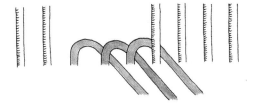

Step 2. Take the first bent-down rod on the left and pass it in front of the next upright stake on the right, behind the next stake and out to the front again. Kink the upright you passed in front of at the same height as the others and then bend it down to join and run parallel with the first bent-down border rod. Don't let them lie on top of one another. There should now be two single and one pair of border rods protruding to the outside of the basket.

Bending down the first border rod to join.

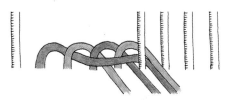

Step 3. Perform the same strokes with the next two bent-down rods and the next two uprights, so that you have three pairs of rods on the outside of the basket.

Three pairs bent down on the outside of the basket.

Step 4. Take the right-hand rod from the left-hand pair of rods and pass it in front of the next two upright rods to the right, behind the next and out to the front again. Bend down the first upright on the left to join and lay parallel with it.

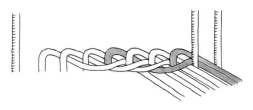

Using the first bent-down rods.

Step 5. Continue with these strokes right around the basket, always using the right-hand rod of the left-hand pair, and leaving the remaining single rod of the pair behind. It will be trimmed off later. When you look more closely at the border you will realize that the right-hand rods on the bent-down pairs are always the least used. These rods, therefore, need weaving in a bit further to make them secure. The left-hand rod of the pair has already completed this stroke and is, therefore, safe to leave.

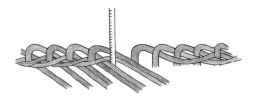

Approaching the end of the three-rod border.

Step 6. The last upright is threaded underneath the elbow of the first bent-down rod and the right-hand rod of the left-hand pair is threaded underneath the elbow to join it. This will leave no upright rods and three pairs remaining on the outside of the basket.

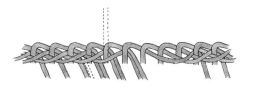

Bending down the last upright on a three-rod border.

Step 7. To finish the border, the right-hand rod of each pair is woven in front of two and behind one, as you have done for the rest of the border. For this last stage of the border, a well-greased bodkin will need to be used. Insert the bodkin where the rod is destined to pass through and leave it there until at least the first 5cm or so of each border rod have been threaded through the gap, then remove the bodkin. Gently ease the

Threading the last rods through the three-rod border.

remainder of the rod through, trying to avoid kinking it.

Five Rods Behind Two Border

This rod border follows exactly the same principle as the three-behind-one border, i.e. laying two parallel rods behind a stake, but it gives a slightly thicker result. Behind-two rod borders are on the whole easier to finish neatly, since the gaps at the ends of the border are not so tight. An even thicker border can be achieved by laying down six or even seven rods at the beginning and weaving them in as you did for a five-rod border. A narrower border is achieved by laying down a four rods behind one or two border.

Step 1. Kink five stakes at an even height above the weaving and bend them down, each behind the next two uprights to the right and out to the front again. Take the left-hand bent-down rod and pass it in front of the next two uprights, behind the next one and out to the front again. Leave it laying quite loosely at the edge of the basket, as this will make it easier to finish the border. Bend down the furthest left-hand upright to join and run parallel with it. Continue this pattern with the remaining single bent-down rods. There should then be five pairs of uprights bent down.

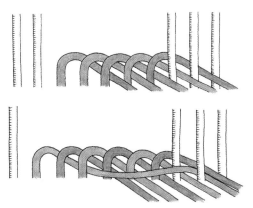

Bending down the first five rods.

Making the first pair.

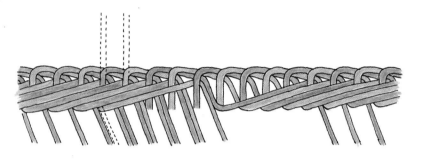

Finishing a five rods behind two border.

Double-rod border.

Step 2. Using a similar method as that described in the three-rod border, use the right-hand rod of the left-hand pair and pass it in front of the next two uprights, then behind one and out to the front again. Bend down the left-hand upright to join and run parallel with it. Continue laying the border down like this until there are just two uprights left.

Step 3. To finish off the border, the remaining uprights are bent down and threaded underneath the elbows of the first two bent-down stakes. The right-hand rods of the furthest two left-hand pairs are threaded in front of four stakes (bent down at the beginning) and behind one. There should be five pairs protrud-ing on the outside of the basket and no uprights left. Pass the remaining right-hand rods of the bent-down pairs in front of four and behind one bent-down upright.

Double-Rod Borders

Double-rod borders are an attractive variation on the rod-border theme. They are woven in the same way as any other rod border, except that they use two rods. As for a plaited border, only try to lay down a double-rod border if the uprights are quite wide apart. To lay down this border, insert an extra stake into the siding beside the existing upright after the side weaving has been finished. Alternatively, use whole rods for bye stakes on the basket inserting them beside the uprights at the upsett. Lay down the rod border as normal, using both rods at once and keeping them flat and parallel to one another. The double-rod border is also easier to lay down when using a behind two-rod border.

Cramming-off a rod border.

CRAMMING-OFF ROD BORDERS
The border can also be finished off by cramming the last weavers. Kink the rod at the point where it would have passed under the border had you been threading it away, and slype the end. Use the bodkin to make a space next to the upright rod it would have passed under and ease the tip of the slyped rod into the gap, being careful not to kink it in other places. Tap the elbow down into position with the rapping iron. The aim is to simulate the finish of the border.

PLAIT BORDERS

The plait border gives a basket a superb finish, and just like the trac and rod borders there are many variations on a theme. Don't attempt to work a plait if the stakes are very close together, the tight angles make it is easy to kink the stakes in the wrong places. At the start of the plait, additional weaving rods are worked in so that the plait is balanced at the finish. False sticks are also temporarily placed at the start to ensure that a gap is left for the final strokes of the border. The false sticks are removed as the finish is approached.

Step 1. Find three rods that are about the same length and width as the uprights above the weaving; and also two sticks 2–8cm long and the same thickness as the butts of the three extra rods. Place a short stick at about 45 degrees and to the right of an upright, bend the upright over it to the right at an angle of about 90 degrees to the short stick. Lay down one of the extra rods parallel to the bent-down upright, with the butt facing inwards and 5cm or so to spare. Lay the second stick over the top of the first pair of rods and at the same angle as the first short stick. Bend the upright over it and lay another extra rod in as before.

Step 2. Taking the left-hand pair, pass them over the right-hand pair and in front of the next upright, leaving them facing

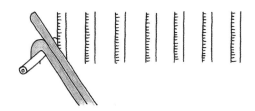

First bent-down rod and inserted stick.

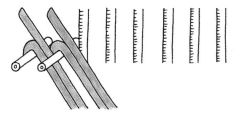

Bending down second upright.

the inside of the basket. Don't pull the first pair of rods too tightly, as plenty of space needs to be left for the rods on the finishing strokes. Avoid kinking them by gently curving them as much as possible.

Step 3. Bend the upright down to the outside of the basket over the rods that now face the inside of the basket, and

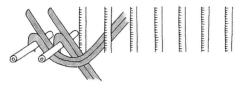

Weaving the first pair on a plait border.

lay the third and final extra rod along side it in the same fashion as the previous two extra rods. There should now be one pair of rods facing inwards and two pairs facing outwards. Taking the left-hand outside pair, curve them over the other pair of outside rods, in front of the next upright stake; leave these also facing the inside of the basket. There should be two pairs on the inside and one pair on the outside.

Step 4. Gently pass the left-hand pair on the inside of the basket, behind the next

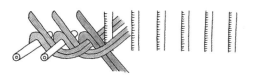

Laying in the third extra rod and weaving the second pair.

upright and over the other inside pair, between the upright stakes and to the outside. Bend the left-hand upright down to join them. There should now be one pair facing inwards, one pair facing outwards, and one set of three also on the outside. Repeat this stage with the last outside pair so that there are two sets of three on the outside.

Step 5. To continue weaving the border,

Weaving in the first and second pairs, bending down the uprights.

stakes are now left behind as in the rod borders. Use the two left-hand rods on the outside and leave the right-hand rods behind each time. It is the most used and most securely woven rod. Taking the left-hand pair on the outside of the basket, pass them over the set of three, in front of the upright, and leave them facing the inside of the basket. Bend the upright over this pair, then bring the inside left pair alongside the bent-down upright. Continue working in this way right around the basket.

Finishing the Plait Border

Step 6. As the end of the border is reached, you will have to begin to take out the temporary short sticks and position the butts of the extra rods as follows. Take a well-greased bodkin and push it in following the route of the first short stick. Leave the bodkin and remove the stick. Take the left-hand pair of the left-hand set of three under the elbow of the upright, following the route of the bodkin. Remove the bodkin when enough of the tips of the rods have been

securely inserted and you are able to pull the rest of them through. Complete the same action with the second short stick.

Starting position for the finish of the border.

Threading the last pairs away.

Step 7. Gently pulling the pairs to the left, pass the ends of the singles to the left and through to the outside of the basket under the border. In doing this you will be simulating the effect on the rest of the border. If you are still not sure where the butt ends go, have a look at the rest of the border and try to copy how it looks. It also helps the passage of the butts through to the other side of the basket if the ends are slyped first.

Threading the butt ends of the extra rods through to the outside.

Step 8. To finish the border, pass the right-hand rod of the inside pairs through to the front, following the passage of the two that already flow in that direction. Either trim off the remaining three rods on the inside or thread them down underneath the border to the outside without letting them show up on the border. Trim off the basket.

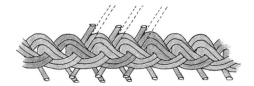

Passing the last rods through to the outside.

Follow-On Borders

A follow-on border makes the rim of a basket much stronger and thicker. Follow-on borders can be made using any bordering technique but they are particularly useful for thickening up narrow borders, such as three-behind-ones or trac borders. After laying down the first border, don't trim the remainder of the uprights off but use them to weave another border underneath the first.

Foot Borders

A foot border is worked onto the base of a basket and is designed to raise its bottom off the ground. It is extremely useful on baskets where the base is likely to undergo considerable wear and tear, e.g. a log basket or a garden basket that is going to spend a lot of time on damp grass. The advantage of a foot border is that it can easily be removed and replaced when it is worn, without interfering with the rest of the structure of the basket. A foot border is not only a good structural device but can look extremely attractive, as well as sometimes successfully hiding a wobbly base!

Plan to put a foot border on at the beginning of a basket by putting on the upsett with a three-rod wale only, starting with tips. This will leave room at the base of the basket for the foot border to be put on at the end. After laying down the border at the top of the basket; turn it over and insert a set of rods into the siding of the basket alongside the uprights. Weave a couple of rounds of waling, if desired, and lay down the border as normal.

Foot border.

8 Handles

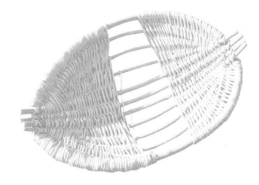

There are endless ways to incorporate handles into a basket. They can either be incorporated into the main structure of the basket or added on at the end. The intended function of the basket usually deter-mines what kind of handle it should have. If, for example, protruding handles would get in the way of storage, then it would be more appropriate to incorporate fingerholes. If a basket is not intended to take a lot of weight, e.g. a flower basket, then strength does not have to be the handle's most important aspect and you can concentrate on its more decorative virtues, whereas in a log basket, strength is all.

FINGERHOLES

Fingerhole handles are openings in the siding of the basket below the border. The border strokes are laid down as normal and the fingerholes incorporated so that, either the border remains level or it is raised up to emphasize the handle positions.

Border Fingerholes
Step 1. These handles are worked as the border is laid down. Use a wide, strong border, if making a bigger basket, to give the border and, therefore, the handles more strength. Before beginning the handles, mark their angle and position on the uprights at opposite points on the basket. Make sure the opening of the handles will not expose the tips of any waling or, if it does, ensure that they are tucked well in, otherwise they will eventually fray loose. Insert bye stakes into the siding weave at the fingerhole points, if desirable or necessary because of thinning uprights.

Step 2. Begin the border at a point where it will run parallel with the top of the weaving, not at a section that will be raised for the fingerholes. As you approach the sections that are to be raised, follow the marks scored earlier. Be careful not to allow the uprights on the raised section to lean to the right as you lay the border down. Continue the border right around the basket and finish as normal. If you feel you need extra width below the handle section, raise the last row of waling too, before putting down the border; but be careful not to make it too wide, as this will make the handles difficult to grip. Also try to ensure that the waling is very tight to prevent it slipping down the uprights.

Opposite: Raised finger-hole in progress.

TIP
Fingerholes can also be made by clever use of packing (see Chapter 7), i.e. add on two or more sections of packing prior to laying down the border as normal. This will give a gently curving fingerhole, whilst maintaining a level border.

Fingerholes made with packing.

Siding fingerholes.

Siding Fingerholes

Step 1. When putting on the siding, calculate in advance how far up the side of the basket the fingerholes should be. Siding fingerholes are made by randing back and forth between stout sticks and leaving a gap in between. There should be enough room after the main siding weave has been put on to allow for this short section of randing, before the top waling is put on.

Step 2. Complete the main siding weave and put on a row of waling. Cut two stout sticks for either side of each fingerhole, slightly longer than the intended height of the fingerhole. Slype the end of the butts and insert them one to the left and one to the right of an upright where the fingerholes will be. The extra sticks will prevent the uprights from distorting as you weave around them. They will give the handles a sturdier appearance and are certainly a useful guide as to where the fingerholes should be left when putting in the randing.

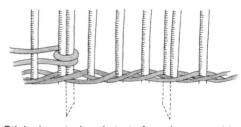

Sticks inserted and start of rand on one side.

Step 3. Starting with the butts at the furthest distance from the designated place for the fingerholes, use fine weavers and rand in between the stout sticks, as you would for a square base, until the desired height has been reached. Put a narrow band of waling on right around the basket, going over the top of the gap created by the fingerholes, and lay down the border as usual.

HANDLE BOWS

As a general rule, the nearer the top of the handle bow to the border, the stronger the handle is. If the basket is not intended to take any notable weight, then feel free to exaggerate the height of the handle to decorative effect; but on a working basket if the handle bow is too high it will tend to wiggle about and become loose. A strong and comfortable handle bow should always be made from a very thick rod. A thick bow will also gives the basket a more balanced appearance. Wood that is too thick to use in any other part of the basket is ideal for the handle bow. If you are intending to use a handle bow, it is important when planning the basket to use handle liners when working up the siding.

Unwrapped Handle Bows

If you have found an attractively coloured and textured, thick and bendy rod, there is no reason at all why it should be covered up with wrapping. On the whole, sticks with a fork or side-shoots are unsuitable, since it is difficult to attain a balanced curve; but occasionally these features can be cleverly used to great effect, so you don't always have to be on the look out for a smooth clean rod. Go for something with a few knobbles and quirks if you think it will bend without breaking.

The stick should be long enough to complete the bow and also reach down

Prepared handle bows.

Inserted handle liners.

HANDLE LINERS
Handle liners are stout sticks inserted into the siding of the basket. Once they are removed there is a ready-made space for the handle bow to slip into. Forcing a handle bow into the siding without having made space with liners first, distorts the shape of the basket. For a single bow, select two sturdy sticks 5cm or more longer than the intended height of the basket. Ideally they should also be just slightly thinner than the width of the handle bow, then when the liners are removed and replaced with the handle bow it will fit nice and tightly into the gap.

through the weaving of both sides of the basket, preferably as far as the upsett. The maximum width of the bow should be no wider than the top of the basket, otherwise it will distort its shape.

Once you have found a suitable rod, gently curve it into a bow shape and tie it in position with tape or string. Leave it in a warm, dry place for at least a week, so that when the bow is untied it doesn't spring back. Be aware of where the belly and the back are on the rod and use this natural tendency to your advantage when bending the bow, i.e. the belly should be on the inside.

Inserting and Pegging the Handle Bow

When the handle bow is in position, slype and put a long taper on the inside of the handle bow (to ease its passage through the siding). Remove the handle liners and insert the bow as far as it will go.

The handle bow now needs pegging into position. Using a bradawl or the point of your bodkin, skewer a small hole or split through the handle bow in between the rows of top waling. Cut a small wedge-shaped peg from a piece of willow or similar, long enough to pass completely through the side of the

Pegging the handle bow.

basket and the handle bow. Tap the tip end of the peg into the hole with the rapping iron and trim off the ends of the pegs with a pair of secateurs.

Rope Handles

A rope handle is much stronger than an unwrapped handle. The handle is wound round with a series of rods, which are then threaded away underneath the border, thus firmly tied into the top of the basket. The handle bow does not necessarily need to be quite as thick as is required for an unwrapped handle, since extra strength and width is going to be created by the wrapping rods.

Step 1. Insert and peg into the handle bow as previously described. Select approximately ten thin rods of about equal length and thickness. They should be at least one and a half times the length of the handle bow. More or fewer wrapping rods will be needed depending on the thickness and height of the handle bow and the thickness of the wrapping rods. Trim the ragged tips and slype the butts on the belly. Run the rods a couple of times through your finger and thumb to make them more pliable, as they will be wrapped at tight angles and this will help to avoid getting kinks in the rods.

Step 2. Ease open a gap with a well-greased bodkin on the left-hand side of the handle bow and insert three or four rods as far as you can with the slype facing the bow. The rods should hug the circumference of the handle bow and each other.

With the rods laying flat next to each other, not clustered or overlapping, wrap them around the bow three times so that they end up on the inside of the bow on the opposite side of the basket. Avoid kinking the rods as you wrap the

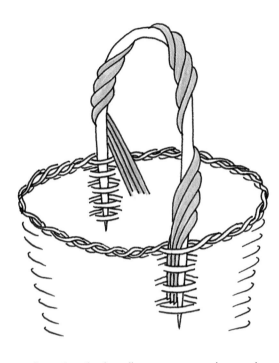

Inserting the handle wrappers and wrapping the handle bow.

bow by taking the tips in wide sweeping movements. Ensure the groups of rods are evenly spaced around the bow.

Step 3. Thread the tips through to the outside of the basket by making a gap in the top waling underneath the border with a bodkin. Complete the same process with another set of four rods on the opposite sides of the basket. When the first two sets of wrapping rods have been put on, use the remaining fine rods to fill in the gaps as needed. Try to use an equal number on each side.

Finishing Rope Handles

There are many ways of finishing off and tying-in a rope handle. Below are illustrations of how to do just a few.

METHOD ONE

Take the group of ends protruding on the outside of the basket diagonally across the front and over towards the inside of

Handle wrappers threaded under the border.

the basket, around the handle bow and back to the outside. Next take them diagonally cross the previous wrap and thread them through the waling again. Pull the wrapping rods as tightly as you can when working the finish. Thread the tips ends in and out under the border through the waling; finishing with the tip ends towards the inside of the basket. Do the same on the other side and trim off the ends with a pair of secateurs.

First stage of method one.

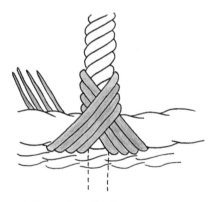

Second stage of method one.

METHOD TWO

Repeat the stokes described in method one but using each rod one at a time at the finish. This method produces an attractive herring-bone effect. I find this method much easier to pull in tightly. Weave the ends away and trim off as in method one.

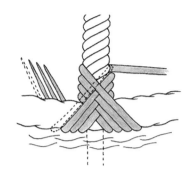

Herring-bone effect (method two).

METHOD THREE

This method is useful if the wrapping rods have finished up on the outside of the basket and they have to be threaded through the waling to the inside of the basket to tie them in. Bring the wrapping rods vertically up and take them right round the front of the handle bow and to the back again. Next take them over to the front again and thread them underneath the diagonal stroke of the wrap, through the waling to the inside of the basket. Weave them away and trim off the ends.

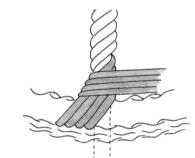

Stage one of method three.

Stage two of method three.

TWISTED HANDLES

Twisted handles are useful for the sides of baskets and on the tops of lids. Although they involve the twisting and breaking up of the grain of the rod, they are still extremely strong, which is why they are invariably put on log baskets.

TWISTED SIDE HANDLES

Step 1. Decide where the handles are to go and insert two untwisted rods on both sides of the border, approximately a hand's width apart. The right-hand rods should be slightly thicker than the left, as they will be used to form the bows of the handles. The left rods will be twisted round the bows first. Bend the right-hand rod to hand height and to the left of the left-hand stick. Thread it through the waling from the outside to the inside.

Step 2. Twist the left-hand rod and wind around the handle bow three times. Thread through to the inside of the basket and to the right of the right-hand stick.

Step 3. Bring the twisted right-hand rod up and wind under the handle and back round to the left again, threading it through to the inside. Do the same with the remaining thicker rod and repeat with the tips ends if there are any gaps left. Weave the tips away through the waling.

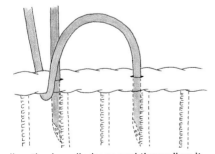

Bending the handle bow and threading it through the waling.

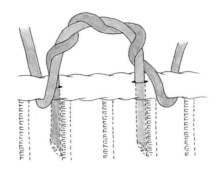

Winding the twisted rod around the handle bow.

The technique is described below as though the handle were being put on top of a lid.

Twisting a willow rod.

TWISTING WILLOW RODS

In order to put on a twisted willow handle, you first have to learn how to twist the rods! The aim of twisting the rods is to render them thong-like, so that they can be wrapped at tight angles without forming kinks. There is a definite knack to this and it will take a little practice. Be careful not to over-twist the rods, as this will make them look ragged. The twisting technique can also be effectively used when working with hedgerow material that would otherwise be too fragile for weaving.

Step 1. Find a perfect rod without cankers or kinks. Slype and insert the rod into the side of the basket, where you wish one side of it to start. Weight the basket down firmly. If it is a large basket just put your foot on the base.

Step 2. The twist is gradually made working down the rod from the tip to the butt. Hold the rod tightly in your left hand a few inches from the tip; this will help to steady the rod and prevent the twist from spreading too quickly and unevenly down the rest of the rod.

Step 3. Crank the tip with your right hand in broad circles until you feel the area of grain between your hands break up. Release your hands and let them slip a little further down the rod, cranking the new area of rod as you go. Don't twist the rod so much that you split it. You can release the areas that have already been twisted with an easy mind, since they are simply wound up again when you come to work the handle.

Small, Single-Rod Handles

Small, twisted handles are useful for the tops of lids and in situations where the handles do not need to be too strong.

Step 1. Only one rod is needed for a small, twisted handle. Trim the tip,

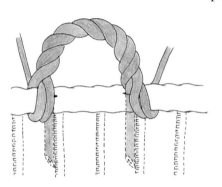

Twisting and wrapping the second rod.

slype the butt and insert it 5cm or so (or a length that is slightly longer than the width of the intended handle) into the top of the lid where you want the handle to be. Use the bodkin to make a gap, if necessary. Kink the butt against the underside of the lid, so that the butt of the rod lays as flush as possible against the weave.

Step 2. Make a bow with the tip end

and thread it to the under/inside at a point that is just before the slype of the butt.

Wrapping the small handle.

Step 3. Pass the tip-end over the butt-end and thread it through to the top of the lid again, pulling it up tightly to secure the butt. The intention is to tie in the butt against the underside of the lid. When the lid is used, the strain on the weave of the lid will be greatly reduced. Wrap the remainder of the rod back and forth over the bow as for the side handles, twisting if necessary and weave away the ends. It is also possible to use a separate stout stick on the underside instead of the kinked butt.

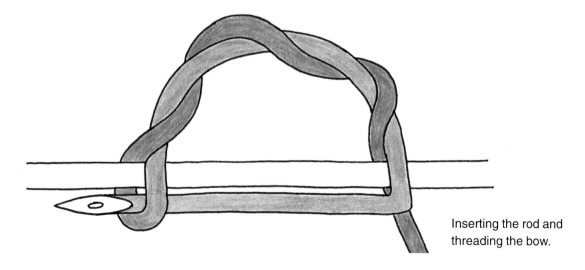

Inserting the rod and threading the bow.

9 Framework

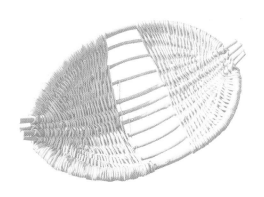

Frame or rib baskets use different methods of construction to those of stake and strand, although they are also ideal for the use of willow and hedgerow materials. The basic frame of the basket is constructed using hoops before the weaving begins, and ribs are added in as work progresses. To make the frame, thick rods are set into shape in a similar way to that used to form handle bows. A huge variety of differently shaped baskets can be made by combining variously shaped hoops and lengths of rib. The set rods are then tied together using skeining and secured in position by the weave of the basket. In contrast to stake and strand work, it is usually the preparation of the frame itself that takes up most of the time; the weaving seeming relatively quick and easy by comparison.

after which, almost any pliable thick wood will do. The hoops and ribs should be made from the thickest willow rods you can find. These will usually be amongst 1.8–2.5m bundles of rods. If using green or hedgerow woods, you will need to shape the hoops and leave them in position for a least a couple of weeks in a warm place before they are set. If using farmed willow, make sure the rods are well soaked before they are bent into shape and hang the hoops up in a warm, airy place until they are thoroughly dried out.

Round Hoops

Using the butt half of a thick rod, bend it round a gas bottle, oil drum, thick post or anything similar and sturdy enough to give you plenty of leverage, and an even and consistent bend. Getting the hoops a uniform size and shape will

Anatomy of a framework basket.

MAKING HOOPS AND RIBS

Farmed willow is easier to make the hoops and ribs with at first until the basic techniques have become familiar;

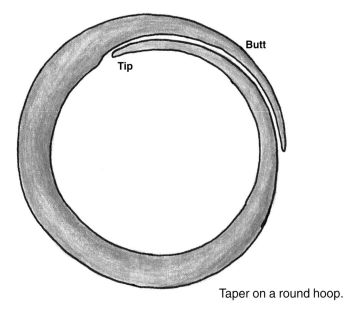

Taper on a round hoop.

help to achieve the desired basket shape. Once the hoop shape has been formed, temporarily release the bow and taper the ends, then re-bend it and tie it into position with a skein (*see* page 79), a piece of string or raffia.

The taper should be at least 8–10cm long, preferably longer. Taper the inside of the rod at the butt end and the outside of the rod at the tip end. This will give you an even width of hoop at the join. When skeining them together, always place the tapered butt on the outside of the hoop. The thick butt is more able to withstand the outward pressure and the hoop and is therefore less likely to distort.

Oval Hoops

Evenly proportioned oval hoops are usually made by joining two bows together. Only try to make an oval hoop with one rod if it is very long, has a very thick girth and has been carefully shaped around a mould and thoroughly dried. Make two bows as you would for a handle bow, bending them round a mould to ensure a consistently shaped curve. The sides of the bows need to be more than half the length of the oval hoop to allow for the taper at the join. When the bows are thoroughly dried

out, taper the insides of the butts and the outside of the tips and join together with a skein.

If using the full length of a willow rod to make a bow, use the tip of the rod as a replacement for string by kinking it up and tying it round at the other side of the bow. Cut the useless cross-piece off when it has dried.

Making Ribs

Ribs can be made with split or whole rods depending on the effect you wish to achieve. Split rods give a flatter surface effect to the weave. The ribs should be made of slightly thinner material than the main hoop. They can be made by tying and setting half ovals as described above, then bending them out into a stiff curved rod once they have dried.

Alternatively, cut a set of soaked or green sticks to the desired length, tie them together with tape or string and bend them into shape before drying. Setting them in a mould to dry is another possibility. The mould could be made using two parallel sets of nails tapped into a piece of hardboard. Slip the intended ribs in between the lines of nails to dry.

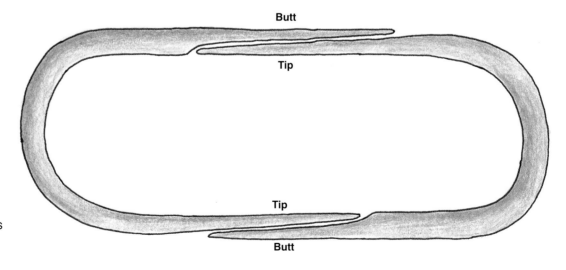

Tapers on oval hoops to be joined.

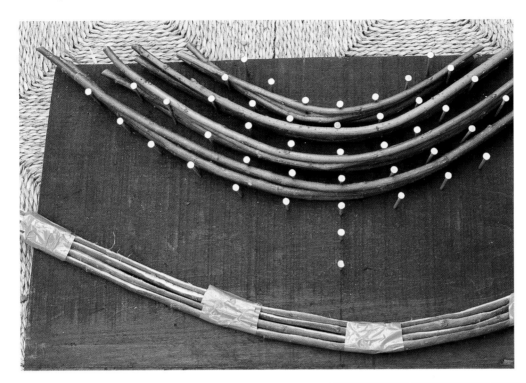

Methods of shaping ribs.

Starting to split a rod.

Splitting Rods and Making Skeins

Skeins are made by splitting whole rods into ribbons and are used in framework to tie in the tapers and join the ribs to the hoop. Skeins are also used on some baskets for wrapping handles.

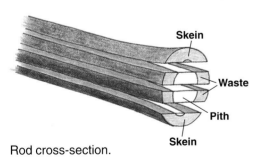

Rod cross-section.

Step 1. Select a soaked perfect willow rod without cankers or kinks and slype the butt end. Using a handknife to start it, cleave the butt end open by pushing the blade across the short width of the slype and levering the grain in half.

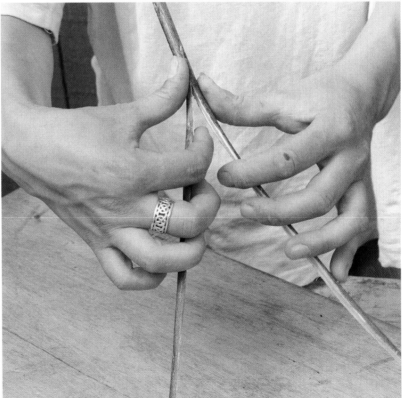

Right: Scraping out the pith.

Step 2. Now comes the tricky bit – it does take time to master but will come with a little patience and practice. The aim is to continue the split along the length of the rod to the tip, keeping the two halves of equal thickness all the way.

Grip the rod under your arm with the butt towards you. Form your thumb and forefinger into a 'A' shape by placing the forefingers on the butt and the thumbs against the remainder of the rod. Pull the split apart with the fingers and control its progress with the thumbs. If one side is becoming thicker than the other, gradually bring the split back to the middle by placing more pressure on the thicker side with the thumb.

Step 3. Once the rod has been split in half, it needs to be quartered! Split each half along its length again in the same way as you did the first time. If the inside frays off, just use the handknife to start it off again and continue along the rod's length. If the outer bark side frays off, you have either just got to hope the skein is already long enough to do the job you require of it, or you will have to start again! The rod quarter should have a ribboned cross-section. It is the two outer halves that form the skein. The inner sections are waste and can be discarded.

Step 4. Once the rod has been quartered, it only remains to take out the last bit of pith. Do this by laying the skein on your knee, inside uppermost. Laying a rag or piece of leather on your knee first to protect yourself and your clothing, lay the blade of your knife vertically against the inside of the skein and pull the skein underneath it all the way along its length; scraping off the pith as you go. When this is done you should have a ribbon-like length of willow to tie the hoops with.

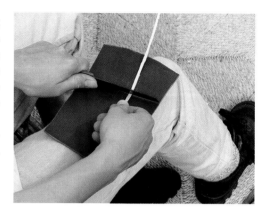

TIP
It is possible to make skeins using the skeining and shaving tools mentioned earlier in the book. However, it is a skill in itself learning how to use these tools effectively, so, unless you plan to make skeins on a large scale, it is cheaper and easier to learn how to make them by hand. If you find skeining rods tricky at first you can use string or raffia to join the hoops together.

Tying In Tapers

To join the two halves of the hoops together, you will have to tie the tapers together with skeins, or something equally strong and fine. Whatever is used, its texture and colour must be compatible with the other materials in the basket, since it may show through once the weaving has been put on the frame.

Overlap the tapers (butt end on the outside) and trap one end of the skein between the two, approximately in the middle of the total length of the taper. Wrap the skein around the hoop to one end of the join, then work back to the middle, crossing the first wrap. Continue to the opposite side of the taper and work back to the middle again. Thread the remainder of the skein between a gap in the centre of the join and trim off the end.

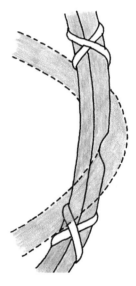

Tying tapers together.

Nick in hoop.

JOINING THE HOOPS

The basic frame of the basket is made by lashing together two hoops with skeins or very fine whole rods. Joining variously shaped hoops at different angles to one another provides the basis for all kinds of shapes. There are many different designs used for lashing the hoops together, a couple of which are illustrated below. If the basket is to have a raised handle, then one-half of one hoop will form its bow.

Lashing

Before beginning the lashing, dip the skeins in water to give them maximum suppleness. Make a small nick in the hoops where they join together. The nick is useful as a marker but it also helps to stop the hoops from sliding around as you tie them together. Slip the butt of the skein between the axis of the hoops, where the nick is if you have made one. Leave 5cm or so of skein to spare at the end of the lashing, so that it can be

covered and secured in with the weave. If putting the lashing on with a fine whole rod, use the remaining end to start the weaving.

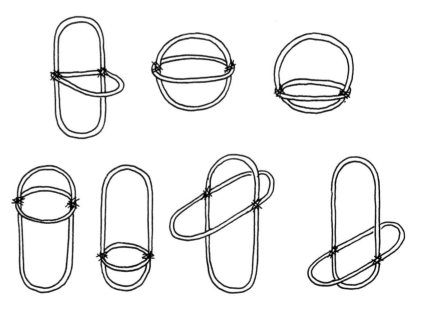

Some potential shapes.

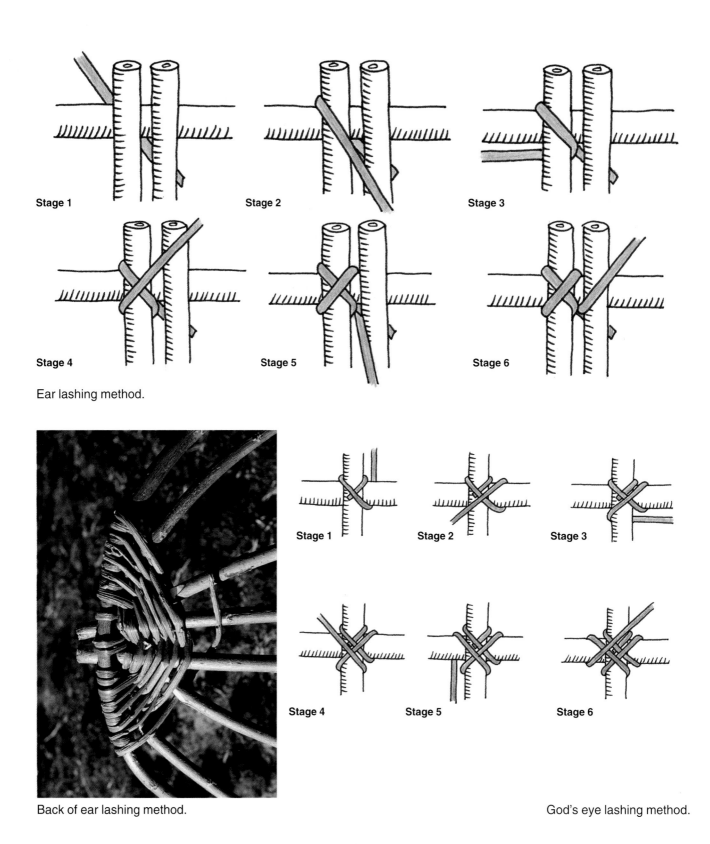

Stage 1 **Stage 2** **Stage 3**

Stage 4 **Stage 5** **Stage 6**

Ear lashing method.

Stage 1 **Stage 2** **Stage 3**

Stage 4 **Stage 5** **Stage 6**

Back of ear lashing method.

God's eye lashing method.

Front of God's eye.

Back of God's eye.

Ear Lashing

The ear lash is the simplest lashing to complete, and most appropriate for use on small baskets and those without handles. Three or four are put on in succession when attaching the initial ribs.

God's Eye Lashing

The God's eye is a very attractive method of joining the hoops, especially when made large. It is most useful on frame baskets with handles, since it makes a pocket for the first ribs to be inserted into.

JOINING RIBS TO THE HOOPS

The hoops determine the main axis but the ribs determine the outline of the basket and are added gradually as the basket is woven up. The first ribs should be added in pairs and positioned so that

  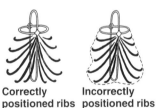

Intended outline **Correctly positioned ribs** **Incorrectly positioned ribs**

Joining ribs to hoops.

they will divide the spaces equally on either side of the main hoops. Subsequent ribs are added into the pockets created by weaving around the first ribs and the main hoops. The ribs should be cut to the right length to make the desired outline before insertion. Unwanted angles may develop as a result of putting in a rib that is too long/short, or protruding at the wrong angle. It may be that you have not put in enough ribs so that a straight line instead of a curve emerges between the ribs.

Attaching Ribs to Baskets with Ear Lashing

On baskets where a raised handle is not part of the main structure, the first ribs are usually attached with an ear lash using a whole or skeined rod. Attach the ribs at either end of the main hoop with a very fine willow rod or skein. This can be fiddly at first since one end of the ribs may move around while you are

Attaching the first ribs by splitting the hoop.

attaching the first side. It will help if you hold one side of the hoop against your stomach and tie the far side in first.

If you find attaching the ribs as described above too tricky, split the rod and insert the ribs through the gap before tying in. Don't cut off the weaver once the first ribs are tied in but rand it around the hoop and ribs until its end, thereby using it as the first weaver. Once the ribs have been tied in with an ear lash, check the positioning and angles of the ribs. It is still possible to adjust them slightly at this stage.

Attaching Ribs to Baskets with an Eye of God Lashing

Handles on frame baskets are often made by utilizing one-half of two main axis hoops joined together by an eye of God lashing. If the basket hoops have been

Adding the first ribs into a God's eye.

joined using a God's eye lashing, insert the first ribs into the pockets made by the God's eyes. Cut the ribs to length and slype the ends so that the point of the slype tucks neatly into the corner of the pocket left by the lashing. Begin randing them securely in place with the butt of a fine weaver. Place the butt on the inside of the handle hoop to start. If the God's eye lashing is too small to securely insert the first ribs, rand back and forth between the main hoops to make larger pockets for the ribs to be fitted into.

WEAVING THE FRAME BASKET

Frame baskets are not woven from one end to the other, as you would for a stake and strand basket, but are woven from both ends of the frame at once so that a narrowing gap emerges in the middle of the work. The weave on a frame basket is a basic rand: weave back and forth between the ribs and around the hoop as you would for a square base, only instead of weaving around end sticks, the rand is woven around the hoop of the frame.

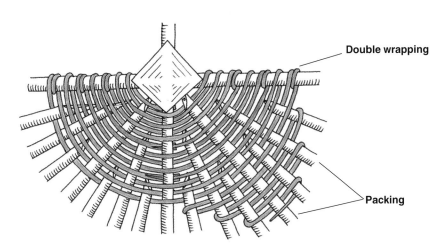

Randing around the frame packing and double-wrapping.

Double wrapping

Packing

Always join in on the inside with the butts of weavers. Try and arrange your weave so that the butts lie in a neat line along the central ribs. The overall effect will be much more even and polished. Avoid laying in new butts too close to the rim of the basket, the strength of the basket will be undermined.

The natural bow in the shape of a frame basket will not allow you to rand along it in straight lines between the outer hoops. On the contrary, the weave on a frame basket would naturally flow in a crescent and leave you with two 'V' shapes unweaved at the end. To counteract this tendency it will be necessary to use packing (*see* pages 57–8) to straighten the lines of weaving, which should be parallel as you approach the finish of the basket.

Double-wrapping around the outer frame as you weave back and forth will also help to even out the weave (*see* page 39). It may not be appropriate to wrap around the outer hoop twice on every occasion but try and keep the double-wrapping even and symmetrical to give the basket a neat appearance. Get the lines of weav-ing straight as soon as possible; this obviates the need for fiddly filling in near the end when the gap for weaving through in the middle of the basket is very small.

As you weave, add more ribs into the emerging pockets besides the existing ribs where necessary. Try to insert all the ribs as soon as possible. You only need to put in enough ribs to outline the shape of the basket and prevent the weave from becoming loose and angular. Place an equal number of ribs in on each side of the basket. Stand back and look at the basket and try to imagine how the weavers will bend around it and where any unwanted angles are likely to develop.

Very well-soaked and mellowed weavers will be needed to fill in the last couple of inches of weaving, since the angles are likely to be tight where the gap is small. Use the bodkin to help you finish off the last couple of rows.

Half-woven frame basket with straightened lines of weaving.

Project 1: Round Larch Basket

This dainty little basket uses a combination of farmed willow and hedgerow materials. It could be used for the collection and storage of either eggs or soft fruits, for example. I have used brown willow for the main frame of the basket and larch branches for the siding and handle, but alternative willows and hedgerow materials could just as easily be used. Larch stems can be very long and pliable, and are one of the few hedgerow basketry materials that can be used straight away without the need for drying them out first. Larch is best collected between December and March, when the myriad of dense feathery leaves have all dropped off.

Materials

- Six sticks 16cm (6–7 inches) long, cut from the butts of the thickest 120cm (4ft) brown willow rods, for the slath.
- Sixteen to twenty fine 90cm (3ft) brown willow rods, for the base pairing.
- Twenty medium-thickness brown willow rods, for the upsett and waling.
- Twenty-four thick, straight, 90cm (3ft) brown willow rods, for the uprights.
- A bundle of about 50 very fine long larch stems, for the siding.
- A thick larch branch approximately 50–60cm (2ft) long, for the handle.
- Two handle-liner sticks, approximately 25cm (10 inches) long.

Method

Step 1. Soak the 90cm willow rods and the six base sticks for two days and mellow them for a few hours or overnight prior to the weaving. When you have made a few bases, it should not be necessary to soak the base sticks for a basket this small, as they are not very long and won't actually need to bend very much; but in the first instance it may be helpful to have the base sticks a little more pliable than is necessary.

Step 2. Collect a bundle of larch branches for the siding and a branch thick enough and pliable enough to form the handle bow. Trim off any side-shoots from the larch stems. Larch branches get blown from the tree very easily in bad weather, so it may be worthwhile looking around on a woodland floor to find as much as you need. If you find any stems with their cones still attached, leave them on and incorporate them into the weave of the basket. I have chosen not to incorporate the cones on this basket, however, as they would get in the way of its function. Instead I looked for pieces of larch that had a few smatterings of moss and lichen attached, to add extra interest.

Step 3. To make the base, use the finest rods you have soaked and mellowed, and the six thick sticks cut from the butts of 120cm rods. Split three sticks

Opposite: Basket and larch material.

and thread the other three through the split, ensuring the belly and the back of the sticks all flow the same way. Begin base pairing with the tips of two of the fine rods. Tie in the slath and open all the base sticks out on the first round of pairing.

Step 4. Continue base pairing with the fine weavers, joining in tips-to-tips and butts-to-butts until a diameter of approximately 15cm has been reached. Spread the base sticks out evenly, as soon as possible, and give the base a slight concave (the finished base should sit on its rim). Finish with tips and tuck the ends away into the previous row of pairing. Trim off the ends of the pairing weavers with a pair of secateurs flush against the base sticks, and the ends of the base sticks flush with the edge of the base. When the base is finished it should rest on its rim and not wobble about.

Step 5. To begin putting on the upsett, slype the twenty-four thickest rods on the back and insert them through the pockets in the weave as far as they will go, one on each side of a base stick. Use the bodkin to make a channel by the base sticks first, if necessary.

Step 6. Using a handknife, prick-up the side stakes as close to the edge of the base as possible, holding them in an upright position with a hoop. Place a weight that won't interfere with your hands when weaving, on the base.

Step 7. Slype eight of the medium-width rods on the belly and trim all the tips so the rods are the same length. Insert four into the weave of the base alongside and to the left of four consecutive uprights; the slype should face the underside of the basket. Put on a four-rod wale (see Chapter 5), pulling down the weavers as close to the edge of the base as possible,

ideally into the crook of the uprights. Continue waling until you have reached the opposite side of the base. Insert the remaining four waling weavers and work these round until the beginning of the first set is reached.

Step 8. Continue a four-rod wale to the tips of the rods by chasing the two sets of weavers around the basket. As you continue the waling, concentrate on evenly spacing the uprights. Don't let any individual upright lean in or out of the basket. Control the upright with the thumb and forefinger of your left hand, while weaving with the right.

Step 9. The upsett is continued using a three-rod wale and only one set of waling weavers, this is to prevent the upsett waling getting too high before the rest of the siding is put on. Trim the butts and tips of the rods so that they are of equal length. Start with tips and join in a single set of three rods, alongside the tips of a set of the previous four-rod waling. Do this by ignoring the tip of the foremost four-rod waling weaver (*see* Chapter 5). As the new walers progress around the circumference of the basket they will travel over the tips of the second set of four-rod waling.

Step 10. Continue with the three-rod wale when you reach the butts by joining in another set, butt-to-butt, leaving the ends either on the inside or the outside of the basket. Weave a wale until you reach the tips of this new set. Tap the weaving down with the rapping iron.

Step 11. Put a long pointed taper onto the thick end of the handle liners and insert them into the upsett on opposite sides of the basket to the left of an upright.

Step 12. At this point stand back and look at the basket to see how the shape is progressing. Straight sides have already been dictated by using uprights that have been slyped on the back, but it is possible to make the basket flow out a little more at the sides. The easiest way to do this is to slide the hoop that holds the uprights in position up a little, or remove it altogether. On your first few baskets, however, it is advisable to leave the hoop on, since it will help to keep an even circumference on the uprights.

Step 13. The larch siding is made using a French rand. Follow the steps on starting a French rand in Chapter 6, using the butt ends of twenty-four larch branches. Two rounds of randing will eventually be put on the siding of the basket. Rand around the handles liners and their parallel uprights as though they were one stake. In this case it doesn't matter if the larch branches aren't of equal length, although it's normally essential when putting a French rand on with willow.

Step 14. Normally in willow basketry the two rounds of randing would have a distinct beginning and end, and a row of waling put on in between them. In this case, however, I have blurred the line between the two rounds so as not to give the effect of two separate rounds on the siding. Rand to the tips of all the larch weavers, adding in the butt of a new larch weaver as one runs out – even though the remaining weavers may not have reached their tips. The second round of randing should finish at roughly the same level on the siding, so when starting to lay in the second set, lay in the longest of the remaining larch branches first, joining in the short lengths when the longest weavers of the first set run out. Hopefully the tips will all finish at the same time at the top!

Step 15. Rap the larch down frequently as the siding progresses otherwise the

knobbles on the larch tend to prevent the weavers laying tightly on top of one another.

Step 16. The basket in the photograph was approximately 14cm high by the time the randing panels had been put on. Don't worry if yours is not exactly this height; variations in the widths and lengths of hedgerow material invariably mean it is impossible to reproduce baskets down to the last centimetre!

Step 17. When the side randing has been finished, a round of waling is put on to strengthen and tidy up the top of the basket. Slype six medium-thickness rods on the belly and trim the tips so that the rods are of equal length. Start a round of three-rod waling with the tips. Continue with the next three rods joining butts-to-butts. Give the basket a final tap down with the rapping iron.

Step 18. Leaving the handle liners in position, follow the instructions for laying down a four or five rods behind two border. I have used a four rods behind two border here.

Step 19. The handle is now prepared. Using the thick larch branch, gently bend it so that the width of the bow is no wider than the top of the basket. The bow above the border should be no more that half the total height of the basket, and the sides of the handle bow should reach down to the upsett. Tie the bow in position with a piece of string and leave it to dry out and set in position for a week or two.

Step 20. Once the bow is set so that it won't spring out when the string is removed, taper the inside ends of the bow. Remove the handle liners and insert and peg the bow into position (*see* Chapter 8). Trim the basket to finish.

Project 2: Round Wild Willow Basket

This general utility basket is made from willow from my own garden (*S. triandra* and *S. fragilis*), but it is just as easily made from commercially bought willow and all the instructions that follow are given as though it were. To make it from your own collected willows, simply collect enough rods of comparable width and length. The willow for this basket was slightly clung, i.e. still partially green and pliable, so there was no need to soak the rods. If you want to use a mixture of commercial willow and collected materials, and you can't find any hedgerow materials as long as the commercially grown willow used for the siding, just cut the butts off the commercial willow so that it is the same length as your hedgerow material; this will help to ensure an even rand when the siding is put on. The basket measures 25cm in height and has a foot border which can be replaced if it undergoes any harsh treatment. For ease of storage I've given the basket fingerholes instead of raised side handles.

Materials

- Eight thick sticks 32–35cm (13–14 inches) long, cut from the butts of 150cm (5ft) willow rods for the slath.
- Four thick sticks 15–18cm (6–7 inches) long, 2–3 times the width of a pencil for the sides of the finger holes.
- 100–120 fine 120cm (4ft) brown willow rods for the base pairing and siding.
- (To alternate the colours select 50–60 each of two different colours.)
- Sixty medium-thickness 120cm (4ft) brown willow rods for the upsett and waling.
- Thirty-two medium-width 150cm (5ft) brown willow rods for the uprights.

Method

Step 1. Soak and mellow all the commercial willow rods and base sticks. Refer to page 15 to see how long each length of willow needs to be soaked for.

Step 2. If using any hedgerow materials, cut all the siding weavers to the same length.

Step 3. Split four slath sticks with a handknife and thread the other four through, ensuring that the bellies and backs face the same way. Tie in the slath starting with the tips, then pair round the slath opening out all the base sticks on the first round of weaving. Continue pairing and trying to get the base sticks opened out to an equidistant radial position as soon as possible, remembering to start giving the base a slight concave as you go.

Step 4. Join in a new pair of weavers when you reach the butts and continue to

Opposite: Round wild willow basket.

Soaking and mellowing the willow rods.

pair around the base joining tips-to-tips and butts-to-butts, until a diameter of approximately 32cm has been reached. Trim all the protruding ends from the base weavers and the ends of the slath sticks flush with the edge of the base.

Step 5. Slype the thirty-two rods you set aside for the uprights on the back and insert one rod on either side of each base stick, slype down as far as it will go. On a larger base, this may be made easier by holding one side of the base securely under the foot.

Step 6. Prick-up the uprights with a handknife close to the edge of the base, and hold in position with a hoop. Put a

weight in the middle of the basket. Since this basket is going to have a foot border (*see* page 87), it is not necessary to have a sturdy four-rod wale for the upsett, as in Project 1. Indeed the bulk of the four-rod wale would be an obstruction in the way of the rods that will be inserted for the foot border. The upsett on this basket is made with three-rod waling and started with tips. The foot border is put on after the rest of the basket has been finished.

Step 7. To start the upsett, select twelve medium 120cm rods from the pile reserved for waling. Trim the tips and butts so that the rods are all the same length. Insert two sets of three rods into the weave beside the base sticks on opposite sides of the basket, each to the left of an upright stake. Put on a three-rod wale with both sets of weavers, remembering to pull the walers down tightly against the edge of the base. Chase the two sets of waling weavers around the basket and when you reach the butts join in new sets, butts-to-butts. Continue waling with the two sets until the tips are reached. Tap down with the rapping iron.

Step 8. Select thirty-two siding weavers: sixteen of one colour and sixteen of another. Lay them in to start a French rand, alternating the colours. In the case of the basket illustrated, a red weaver was laid next to a green weaver, then another red weaver, and so on. Be sure to maintain this pattern when you come to lay in the last two weavers (*see* Chapter 6). Alternating the colours of the weavers at the start of the rand will create a vertical pattern on the siding.

Step 9. Rand the weavers up to the tips letting the basket flow out a little, while keeping the uprights relatively parallel. Tap down the weave with the rapping iron and put on a round of waling, starting and finishing with tips. Rap the weave down again.

Step 10. Decide where the fingerholes are to go. They should be at least a hand's width wide and at directly opposite points on the basket. Shave tapers at least 5cm long on the thick ends of the fingerhole sticks and insert them down into the weave of the siding, one on the left and one on the right of an upright stake for each fingerhole (*see* Chapter 8).

Step 11. Select around twenty-four siding weavers and rand on both sides in between the stout fingerhole sticks, as

you would for a square base (*see* Chapter 4), until the rand above the waling is approximately 8cm high. Treat the fingerhole stick and its parallel upright as one stake. Double-wrap tightly around the sticks occasionally to keep the randing level and ensure that you don't leave large gaps in the wrapping around the stick.

Step 12. A round of waling is now put on the top of the basket, passing over the top of the gap left by the fingerholes. Starting and finishing with tips, chase two sets of three-rod waling around the basket. Be careful to keep the waling tight and the uprights vertical as you pass over the fingerholes. Join in the butts in the middle of a solid section of siding and avoid joining in the butts of the second set of walers over the fingerholes, as this will create a weak spot.

Step 13. Trim the top of the fingerhole sticks flush with the top of the waling and lay down a plait border following the methods described in Chapter 7. Trim off the remainder of the uprights, which fan round the circumference as a result of laying down the plait, and keep them to one side; they will be used for the foot border.

Step 14. Turn the basket upside down so that it rests on its border. Slype the butts of the remainder of the thirty-two uprights you trimmed from the border. Using the bodkin to make a space, if necessary, insert them down through the weave of the siding, each one alongside an upright.

Step 15. Using one set of weavers only, put on a round of waling from tips-to-butts and butts-to-tips. Lay down a four-behind-two border. Finally trim off all the loose ends from around the basket. Finished!

Project 3: Round Willow Tray

This willow tray is made from a mixture of commercially available buff willows and wild growing *S. fragilis*. It could just as easily be made from other types of willow of comparable width and length. The wild growing willow needs to be collected in the winter when the sap is down and allowed to cling for two or three weeks before it is used. This project instructs you on how to open out a larger numbers of slath sticks. It also presents you with the new challenge of putting a French rand on a base and keeping the round base flat! It has a foot border and raised fingerholes for handles. Apart from its obvious functional uses, it also looks attractive hung as a wall feature.

Materials

- Fourteen straight wild willow sticks approximately 50cm (20 inches) long and 0.5–1cm (1 inch) thick for the slath.
- Twenty-eight long, fine wild willow rods 60–90cm (2–3ft) long for the base randing.
- Forty to fifty fine 90cm (3ft) buff willow rods for the base pairing and randing.
- Thirty-six thick 90cm (3ft) buff willow rods for the base waling and upsett.
- Fifty-six medium-thickness 120cm (4ft) buff willow rods for the uprights.

Method

Step 1. Soak all the buff rods for 2–4 hours or overnight, and mellow. The base sticks and wild willow weavers will not need soaking as they should still be pliable enough to bend.

Step 2. Select seven of the base sticks and put a slit in them with a handknife. Slype one end of the remaining seven and insert them one at a time through the slits of the others. Tap the first stick you insert down to one side of the slit to help make room for the others to pass. Make sure the thick and thin ends of all the base sticks are alternately arranged and that the bellies and backs all flow the same way.

Step 3. Select two fine 120cm buff willow rods to start the pairing with and trim the frayed ends so that the rods are the same length. Though it is large, the slath is still tied in the same way as you would for a smaller base. Tie in the slath, starting with the tips of the weavers.

Step 4. Since there are a large number of base sticks, they cannot be opened out into singles on the first round of pairing. After tying in the slath, continue to use the pairing weavers to open out the base sticks in sets of two and threes, with the group of three base-sticks at the centre of the side (*see* Chapter 4). Since the round base is going to form the main part of a

Opposite: Round willow tray.

tray, endeavour to keep the base as flat as possible when putting on the rest of the base weaving.

Step 5. Continue pairing round the base sticks in sets of two and three, joining in the pairing weavers where necessary, until the width of pairing surrounding the slath is approximately 4–5cm wide. Single all the base sticks out with the next round of pairing .

Step 6. Put on a round of waling, using six of the thicker 90cm base weavers. Starting and finishing the waling with tips. The waling round will separate the base pairing from the randing, which you are now about to put on.

Step 7. The base of the tray is very broad and you will probably need to put on two rounds of randing in order to reach the desired width. In order to make continuous segments of colour, I

decided not to put a row of waling on in between the two rows of randing.

Step 8. Cut the butts from all the buff randing weavers, so that they are the same length as the collected wild willow and trim the tips so that there are no frayed ends. Select fourteen of the buff rods and fourteen of the wild willow rods, and lay them in butts first to start a French rand. Lay the colours in alternately at the start in order to achieve the different coloured segments.

Step 9. Proceed by weaving a French rand all the way to the tips, taking care that the base sticks remain at equal distances apart and that you keep the base flat. You may find it difficult to juggle all the protruding randing weavers whilst putting on the first couple of rows but it will get easier after the beginning of the rand has been woven in and the length of the weavers gets shorter.

Starting the French rand on the tray base.

Step 10. When the tips of the first round of weavers are reached, leave them on the underside of the basket and lay in another row of weavers, butts first. Start a second round of French randing, ensuring that the alternate colours are laid in so that they will continue the pattern. Proceed with the second round of French randing until the width of the base is approximately 45cm across. When this width is reached leave the tips of the weavers on the underside.

Step 11. Finish the base by chasing two sets of three-rod waling around the circumference. Use the thick 90cm buff rods reserved for the base waling and start the two sets with the tips on opposite sides of the base. Join in butts-to-butts when the waling weavers run out and finish with the tips of the next round of chased walers. Leave all the ends on the underside when weaving and trim off all the protruding ends so that they sit flush with a base stick.

Step 12. Having finished the base, put on the upsett by slyping the back of all the rods reserved for the uprights and inserting them into the base as far as they will go, one on either side of a base stick, slype down. Use the bodkin to aid you, if necessary. Prick-up and hold the uprights in position with a large hoop.

Step 13. It is necessary to put a foot border on the tray in order to make the large flat base sit more evenly. The upsett, therefore, is started with tips. Take the twenty-four remaining waling weavers, trim off any frayed ends and cut them to an equal length.

Step 14. Four sets of three-rod waling are chased around the basket (*see* page 42). Insert four sets of three tips to the left of the uprights at equal distances around the base. Chase the waling around until you reach the butts, i.e. wale with the first set until you meet the beginning of the second set, drop the first set and wale with the second until you meet the beginning of the third, and so on. Remember to pull the waling weavers as close to the edge of the basket as possible to avoid leaving any gaps.

Step 15. The main reason for putting as many as four sets of waling weavers on the upsett is so that there will be a consistent length of rod with which to define the position of the handles. When the butts of the first sets of walers have been reached, plan the position of the raised fingerholes. Mark the position and heights of the handles with a pencil, making sure that the start and the finish of the handle width lies between and not above the joins of the waling. Ensure the handle width and height are large enough to fit your fingers through comfortably. The four handles should be opposite each other and at equal distances around the circumference.

Step 16. Join in another four sets of three-rod waling weavers onto the butts of the previous sets and begin chasing them round. Weave the waling rods up and down along the lines of the handle positions that have been marked with a pencil as you go. Continue until the tips are reached. The positions of the handles should be clearly visible.

Step 17. Lay down a plait border above the waling, taking care that the uprights don't lean to the right as you plait over the handles. Use the trimmed remainder of the uprights from the top border to put on a foot border. Take care when inserting the foot border uprights that they do not show up in the space left for the handles. Trim off any remaining ends. The tray is now finished.

Project 4: Oval Mallow Basket

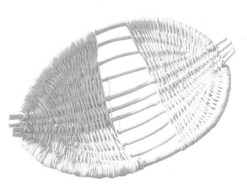

This basket has been designed for use in the garden. It uses an oval base and you should refer to this section of the book to remind yourself how the techniques vary from those of round bases. The basket has a foot border, which can be replaced when worn, and ends that flow out slightly, enabling easy access to garden tools and produce. It is made with a combination of commercially grown brown willow, hedgerow willow and *Lavetera* or Tree Mallow prunings from the garden, which gives the siding an attractive hint of green and purple.

Tree Mallow is too brittle to use immediately after cutting but becomes more pliable if left to dry out for a couple of weeks prior to use. However, it does need to be used up quite soon afterwards, since it quickly becomes brittle again if left too long. The Tree Mallow should be cut in the depths of winter when the plant is dormant and the sap is down. All the same, it may not shed its leaves in the winter if it grows in a milder climate. Either pick off any remaining leaves prior to weaving the stems into the basket, or leave them to dry on the stems and weave them in, as I have done to create a rough rustic effect. If you don't have Tree Mallow available, experiment with the stems of other garden shrubs instead.

Materials
- Four long thick sticks approximately 35–40cm (14–15 inches) in length cut from the butts of 150cm (5ft) willow rods for the slath.
- Seven short, thick sticks 20–24cm (9–10 inches) long cut from the butts of 150cm (5ft) willow rods, also for the slath.
- Twenty-four to thirty-two 90cm (3ft) brown willow rods for base pairing.
- Thirty-four straight, thick 120cm (4ft) brown willow rods for the uprights.
- Twenty-four fine, brown 120cm (4ft) willow rods for the waling.
- A bundle of at least thirty-four Tree Mallow stems approximately 90cm (3ft) long for the siding.
- A thick, bent rod of willow 40–50cm (16–20 inches) long for the handle bow.
- Eight fine 120cm (4ft) willow rods for the handle wrapping.

Method
Step 1. Collect the hedgerow material at least two weeks prior to making the basket and leave it to cling in a dry sheltered position. Soak and mellow the willow.

Step 2. To begin the base, slit the short sticks and slide them into position over the long sticks so that there are three short sticks in the middle and a group of two sticks at each end. Space the single sticks and pairs approximately 4cm (1–2

Opposite: Oval mallow basket.

inches) apart, make sure the middle stick on the group of three is directly in the centre of the slath.

Step 3. The whole base is constructed by continually chasing ordinary reverse pairing weavers until the desired base size is reached. The slath is tied in using the same methods.

Select four fine rods from the bundle of soaked 90cm rods and insert two pairs of tips into the slits on opposite sides of the end slath-sticks. Begin by starting a round of ordinary pairing with one pair of the weavers. When you reach the beginning of the second set, temporarily leave the first set and begin weaving a round of reverse pairing. Revert back to ordinary pairing when you once again reach the first set of pairing weavers. Pair round the slath twice to secure it in position before beginning to open out the base sticks.

Step 4. Open out and separate the ends of the long sticks into a fan shape. As you weave the base, concentrate on stopping the natural tendency of an oval base to twist. Keep the two types of pairing weave close to the slath and the base sticks parallel. Join in new weavers butts-to-butts and tips-to-tips where necessary, always on the long side of the base and never on the fanned end. Continue pairing and reverse pairing around the slath until the end sticks are fully opened out and the base is approximately 20cm (8 inches) wide. Finish the base weaving with a set of tips and trim off the base.

Step 5. Select the willow rods soaked for the uprights and slype them on the belly. Using a bodkin, if necessary, insert them into the base weaving; two on either side of the fanned end-sticks and one alongside each of the short side-sticks, on whichever side will make the

uprights roughly equal distances apart. Prick up the uprights and keep them in position with a hoop.

Step 6. Select twelve of the 120cm brown willow rods reserved for the upsett waling. The upsett is put on with a three-rod wale, starting with tips. Trim all twelve rods to the same length, ridding them of any frayed ends. Insert the tips of six of the waling rods into the base on opposite sides of the basket and start chasing the two sets of waling. Join in with the remaining six waling weavers when you reach the butts and wale to the tips. Rap down the weaving with the rapping iron.

Step 7. Insert two handle liners into the waling each to the left of an upright at directly opposite points on the long sides of the basket.

Step 8. Select thirty-four of the Tree Mallow stems, ensuring that each one will reach around the whole circumference of the basket and that the butt ends are no thicker than the uprights. Put on a round of English randing with the Tree Mallow, passing over two rods on the first stroke to emphasize the spiral (*see* Chapter 6). Keep the long sides relatively vertical but allow the short ends of the basket to flow out as you weave the randed siding. Rap down the weave with a rapping iron.

Step 9. Use the remaining rods reserved for waling to chase around two sets of three-rod waling, starting and finishing with the tips of the rods. Rap down.

Step 10. Lay down a five behind two rods border, treating the handle liner and its parallel upright as one (*see* Chapter 7). Trim off the remainder of the uprights and use them to put a foot border on the underside of the basket.

Step 11. Using a handknife, put a long, pointed taper on the inside ends of the handle bows. Remove the handle liners and insert the bows. With a bradawl, skewer a hole right through the handle bow between the rows of top waling and tap in a willow peg.

Step 12. Select the rods reserved for handle wrapping and trim the butts and tips so that they are all the same length. Working with the natural curve of the rods run them each between your finger and thumb to break up the grain a little and make them more pliable. Slype them on the belly.

Step 13. Insert the slyped ends of the rods in groups of four to the left of each side of the handle bow and wrap them around the bow three times. Finish the handle wrapping with any of the methods described on pages 74–5. Weave the ends of the wrapping rods away and trim of all the protruding ends from around the basket.

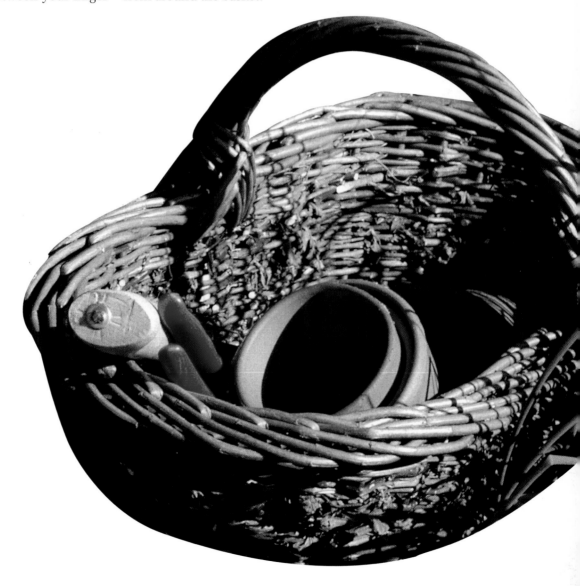

Project 5: Oval Spruce Basket

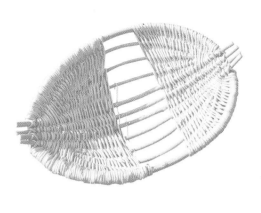

This oval basket is made using commercially grown brown willow and fine spruce stems. The spruce is evergreen and the stems need to be cut several weeks before use to allow all the fine needles to drop first. It may be easier to find sufficient material from the forest floor. The siding of the basket is put on using a version of a 'slewing' weave. 'Packing' is used to raise the height of the basket at the back.

Materials

- Four long, thick sticks 40–45cm (16–17 inches) in length cut from the butts of 150cm (5ft) brown willow rods, for the slath.
- Eight shorter, thick sticks 30–35cm (12–14 inches) in length cut from the butts of 150cm (5ft) brown willow rods, for the slath.
- Sixteen to twenty fine 120cm (4ft) brown willow rods for the base pairing.
- Thirty-six medium-width, straight 150cm (5ft) brown willow rods for the uprights.
- Fourteen medium-thickness 120cm (4ft) brown willow rods for the upsett and waling.
- A large bundle of spruce side stems which have dropped their needles.

Method

Step 1. Soak and mellow the willow rods and shake off the loose needles from the spruce stems.

Step 2. Put a split in the short base-sticks and slide them over the long sticks to make the slath. Arrange four of the short sticks in the centre of the long sticks approximately 2–3cm apart and two pairs approximately 12–13cm from the ends of the long sticks.

Step 3. The base is made by chasing ordinary and reverse-pairing weavers. Begin by inserting the tips of two pairs of weavers in opposite positions through the slit in the slath of the end sticks (*see* page 37). Chase two sets of ordinary and reverse pairing weavers around the slath for two rows and then begin to open out the end sticks.

Step 4. Continue chasing the weavers until the width of the base is complete; joining tips-to-tips and butts-to-butts. The final base should measure approximately 40 cm long and 30cm wide.

Step 5. Select the rods reserved for the uprights and slype them on the belly. Insert them into the base, two on either side of the fanned end-sticks and one by each of the short side-sticks; ensure that the uprights inserted by the short side-sticks are evenly spaced. Kink up the rods and secure in position with a hoop.

Step 6. Select eight of the rods reserved for the upsett and waling. Prepare the rods for the upsett by trimming them, so that they are all the same length, and

Opposite: Oval spruced basket.

slyping them on the butt. The upsett is put on at first using a four-rod wale. Insert two sets of four rods into the weave of the base at opposite points on the long sides of the basket: one rod each to the left of a base stick.

Step 7. Begin chasing two sets of four-rod waling; remember to pull the waling rods well down into the elbows of the uprights on the first round so that no gaps are left between the siding and the base. Reduce the sets of waling weavers from a four-rod wale to a three-rod wale when the start of each set is reached again, by abandoning the foremost waling weaver (*see* Chapter 5). Continue weaving a three-rod wale until you reach the tips again. Tap down the weave with a rapping iron.

Step 8. As the spruce rods are so small and fine, the slewing I have used for the siding of this basket is not put on in the conventional way. Instead, 'clumps' of spruce weavers are used as though they were one rod. The spruce stems are all woven in starting with butts, so that the attractive naturally formed tips can be left protruding on the outside. Start the siding weave as you would for ordinary slewing: rand with one stem to start then two together, three, four, and so on. When reaching the opposite side of the basket, begin chasing a second set of stems in the same way, ensuring that one set of slewing weavers passes in front, and one set of slewing weavers behind, the uprights. Continue until you reach the beginning of the first set again.

Step 9. The width of the slew has gradually increased on the first round of weaving and it is now possible to start weaving in clumps of stems without creating the impression of a sudden increase in bulk. Continue working the slew until it is 4–5cm in height; this will be the lowest point on the basket. Instead of adding one rod each time a tip runs out, add in a group of two or three butts. Ensure that the bulk of the grouped weavers does not outweigh the upright. If a stem has several side-shoots on it, leave them on and weave them as one rod.

Step 10. To raise the height of the basket at one side, follow the method described in Chapter 6. Use a slewing weave whilst putting on the packing. When wrapping round a stake on the packing, i.e. changing direction, abandon the bulk of the weavers and leave them on the outside, wrapping only with a couple of stems to avoid an ugly 'step'. Add in the butts of more weavers once you begin weaving in the opposite direction again. Continue packing until one side of the basket is roughly 12–13cm in height.

Step 11. Rap the slewed spruce stems well down and put on a round of waling, chasing two sets of rods and beginning them both with butts, on the long sides of the basket. Be careful when waling around the ends to make sure you achieve a symmetrical curve. Continue until you reach the tips and tap the work down well with a rapping iron.

Step 12. The basket illustrated has a six rod behind two border but you could use any other border instead. If you have used the measurements indicated, it may be difficult to lay down a plait border, since the uprights will probably be too close together to lay down a plait without kinking the rods. To put on a six rod behind two border, lay down six successional rods behind two rods to the right first, then follow the principles of laying down any other behind two rod border (*see* Chapter 7). Trim off the remainder of the uprights and the inside of the basket. Leave a quantity of tips remaining decoratively on the outside.

Project 6: Squarework Honeysuckle and Bramble Basket

This basket is made with a combination of brown willow, honeysuckle and bramble, which can both be extremely long and pliable; they are prepared prior to weaving by stripping the bramble of its thorns and the honeysuckle of its bark but other than this they can be used immediately after cutting. It is difficult to indicate how much honeysuckle and bramble you will need to cut for the basket, since they all grow at different rates and in different ways. I have estimated the quantity required in centimetres by counting how many times the material travels across the base, which is 30cm wide. It is not necessary to trim the side-shoots off the material, since they can be incorporated into the weave, giving the impression of a slew. The butt ends of the honeysuckle and bramble should be no thicker than the butt end of a 90cm willow rod or half a pencil thickness.

The basket is made using some simple squarework techniques and you will need a screwblock to complete it. If you don't already have a screwblock, they are easily made – take a look at Chapter 3 for instructions on how to make one. Also, take another look at pages 37–8, since this basket is made using many of the same methods as those used to make square bases and lids.

Materials

- Eight brown willow sticks 30–35cm (12–14 inches) long and approximately 1cm (½ inch) thick, cut from the butts of 180 cm (6ft) rods for the base sticks.
- Two willow rods or pieces of doweling 30–35cm (12–14 inches) long and 1.5–2cm (1 inch) thick, for the outer base sticks.
- Sixteen to twenty fine 90 cm (3ft) brown willow rods for the end border and ties.
- One thick 120cm (4ft) brown willow rod for the handle bow.
- Fine lengths of bramble 4–6 m (16–20ft) long, for base weaving and handle.
- Fine lengths of honeysuckle 14–16 m (40–50ft) long, for base weaving and handle.

Method

Step 1. Soak and mellow the 90cm willow rods for the end border and ties and the 120cm rod for the handle bow. Meanwhile collect the honeysuckle and bramble (remembering to take some tough garden gloves with you when collecting the bramble).

Step 2. Prepare the bramble for weaving by first stripping it of its thorns. Put on a

pair of garden gloves and run each length through a tough rag from butt-to-tip and then the other way around.

Step 3. The honeysuckle is prepared by first boiling it in a large pan and then stripping off the loosened bark. Collect two or three lengths of honeysuckle together, coil them up and put them in a pan. Repeat with as much of the remainder of the honeysuckle as is possible to get in the pan and cover it all with water. Cover the pan, bring it to the boil and then simmer it for at least half an hour. The bark should then tease off relatively easily when rubbed with a rough cloth.

Step 4. Set the screw block so that the gap is slightly narrower than the width of the thinnest stick. Using a strong handknife, slype the thick and thin ends of all base sticks alternately and insert the slyped ends into the screw block so that the two thick outer sticks lie 30cm apart and the remaining thinner sticks are evenly spaced in between. Tighten the screwblock and tap the sticks well down into the block so that they don't move around.

Step 5. Weave half-way up the base with the bramble and honeysuckle, using the same methods as you would to make an ordinary square base. Each time you start weaving with a new butt use cramming to conceal it (*see* Chapter 6). Weave the material, along with its side-shoots, as though it was one rod. You may end up weaving bunches of bramble and honeysuckle together, giving a slightly slewed effect. Tap the work gently down with a rapping iron at regular intervals.

Step 6. On reaching the half-way point leave your current base weavers protruding beyond the outer stick. Cram

start another set of weavers. Weave these over to the opposite side of the basket, then leave them also protruding beyond the outer stick, on the opposite side of the base. These weavers will later form the handle wrappers when the handle bow has been placed into position.

Step 7. Continue weaving the second-half of the base with the bramble and

Opposite: Honeysuckle and bramble basket and material.

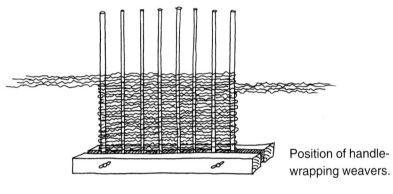

Position of handle-wrapping weavers.

Base tied with string.

honeysuckle until the desired height (the same above, as below, the handle wrappers) has been reached. Rap the weaving down. Remove the base from the screwblock and trim off any protruding ends of the weavers and the ends of the base sticks flush against the weaving. Carefully bend the base into the curved shape so that it is balanced and even, and tie it into position temporarily with string.

TIP

If necessary, give the hedgerow material a little twist (*see* page 75 for tips) to break up the grain prior to wrapping it round the outer sticks. The twist will help you to bend the material at a sharp angle without snapping it.

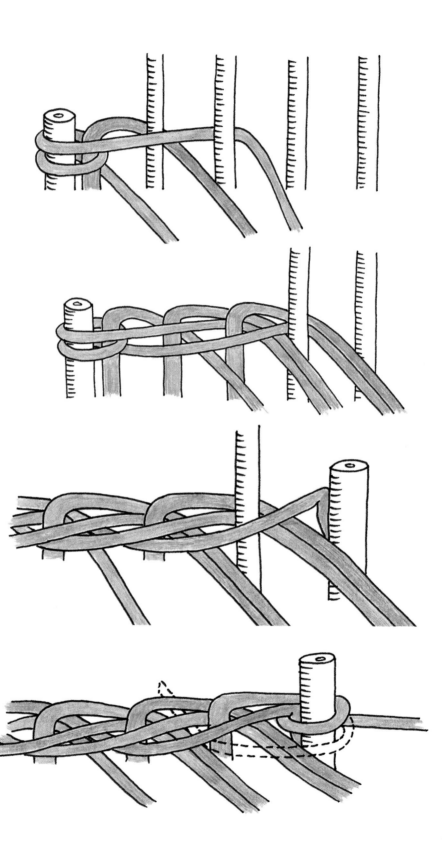

Starting the end border stage one.

Starting the end border stage two.

Finishing the end border stage one.

Finishing the end border stage two.

Step 8. Select the rods reserved for the end border and ties, and slype them on the back or the belly. Insert one rod beside all of the inside base-sticks and one rod to the right of the left-hand outer stick. Use the bodkin to make a channel first.

The start of a three rod behind one border is now simulated. Wrap an extra rod around the left-hand outer stick and its new parallel rod. Bend the rod, which has been inserted by the outer stick, down behind the next stake to the right. Using the left-hand half of the rod, which was used to wrap the outer stick, pass it in front of the next stake to the right, behind the next and out to the front again. Continue by laying down the three-rod border, as you would normally, until you reach the other side (*see* Chapter 7).

Step 9. The end of the three-rod border is simulated when there is only one upright left on the right-hand side. Cram the next weaving rod on the left into the gap to the left of the right-hand outer stick. Kink and wrap the remaining upright around the outer stick and thread it under the elbow of the crammed rod. Wrap it around the outer stick again and thread it away underneath the border behind the next stake to the left. Repeat this three-rod border on the other end of the base and trim off the ends.

Step 10. To secure the border in position it is necessary to attach a tie on both sides of the ends. Insert the butt end of another rod alongside the stakes that are closest to the outer sticks. Twist the rod and wrap it over the border, and two or three layers of the weaving, a couple of times before threading it away to the tips on the main panel of weaving. Put on another three ties in the same way on the other corners of the base.

Step 11. Now it only remains to attach the handle. Select the rod reserved for the handle bow. Slype the butt of this rod on the belly and thread it into the weave, across the base, where it will run parallel with the protruding weavers you have left to form the handle wrappers, i.e. at a central point on the base.

Thread the handle rod through to the outside of the base and pass it over the top of the outer stick to the other side of the base, over the top of the other outer stick and back into the weave of the base from the outside to the inside. Leave sufficient length over the top of the base to form a slight bow. Weave the remainder of the rod back over the handle bow to the other side again, through the base from the inside to the outside and weave the tip away into the weave.

Use the protruding rods reserved for the handle, wrapping with them randomly back and forth over the bow and through the weave of the base until their length is used up. Weave any remaining tip end away into the base weave and trim off the basket.

Project 7: Squarework Willow and Rush Basket

The frame of this small squarework basket is made with brown willow and the siding with a plait of *Monbretia* and Soft Bog Rush stems. The plait could also be made using commercially available basketmaking or chair-seating rush, or any of the leafy stemmed materials mentioned on page 00. As the plait used is quite thick, small byes takes are also inserted into the upsett and are also used to lay down a trac border, along with the main uprights.

Materials

- Eight thick sticks 25–30cm (10–12 inches) long, cut from the butts of 180cm (6ft) brown willow rods, for the base sticks.
- Twenty to thirty fine 120cm (4ft) brown willow rods, for the base randing.
- Thirty-two 120cm (4ft) brown willow rods of medium thickness, for the uprights
- Thirty-two brown willow tips approximately 30cm (12 inches) long, for the bye stakes. Trimmed-off remainders of border uprights are useful for this purpose.
- Eighteen fine 120cm (4ft) brown willow rods, for the waling.
- An armful of dried *Monbretia* and Soft Bog Rush, sufficient to make two 180cm (6ft) lengths of plait approximately 2cm (½ inch) wide.

Method

Step 1. Prepare the materials for the plait by collecting and drying the leaf stems using the method described on page 18. When the stems are thoroughly dried, sprinkle them with water using a watering can and wrap them in a damp cloth overnight to mellow. The stems should then be ready for use.

Step 2. Soak and mellow the willow rods. The base sticks don't need soaking.

Step 3. Start the plait by looping a bunch of stems over a nail, which will help you to keep the plait tight. Lay a third bunch of stems in between the two and begin plaiting with the three groups. Keep the plait even and continuous by adding more stems into a thinning group, butt first, when a tip from the group runs out. Conceal the start of the butt by ensuring that it is laid in where another group will plait over it.

Continue to plait in this way until approximately 3.5–4m of plait has been made. This is more than you'll need but it is better to have too much than too little, as it's difficult to add more plait to the siding later if you find you haven't made

Opposite: Willow rush basket.

enough in the first place. Cut the plait in half to make two separate lengths.

Step 4. Begin the base by slyping and inserting the base sticks into the screwblock. Make sure the thick and thin ends of the sticks are alternately arranged. Position the sticks so that there are two pairs lying 20cm apart and the remainder of the base sticks are evenly spaced in between.

Step 5. Select the rods reserved for the base randing and weave up the base until it is 22–25cm long. Remove the base from the screwblock and trim off the butt ends and tips from around the base, so that they lie flat against the base sticks. Cut the ends of the base sticks flush against the edge of the weaving.

Step 6. Select the rods reserved for the uprights and slype them on the belly. Insert eight rods into each of the short ends (including the ends of the outer base sticks) and seven into each of the long sides, (*see* Chapter 5). Prick-up all the rods with a handknife and secure with a hoop.

Step 7. Select twelve of the willow rods reserved for waling. Put on the upsett waling by chasing two sets of three-rod waling around the basket, starting and finishing with the tips of the rods. Join the new butts in on the long sides and not the short ends. Begin the two sets by looping the tip ends of the waling rods around a central upright on the long sides and working the rods out to their waling position then continue as normal.

Ensure that, as you weave around the ends of the base, you pull the weavers well down into the elbows of the uprights, so that no gaps are left between the edge of the base and the upsett. Tap down the waling weave when you reach the tips again.

Step 8. Insert one end of a plait behind a stake and rand it half-way round the basket. Leave the plait hanging outside the basket, in front of a stake. Insert the end of the second plait behind the same stake. Rand the second plait around the other half of the basket. Continue by chasing and randing both plaits around the basket, so that the one plait always passes in front and one passes behind the same stake, until three or four layers have been woven around the basket. Allow the basket to flow out slightly as you weave; be sure to keep the corner stakes in the correct position as you weave around them with the plait. Don't allow them to lean to the left or right but try to keep them parallel with the rest of the stakes. Finish weaving the two plaits on opposite sides of the basket.

Step 9. Select the remaining waling rods and lay in two sets of three-rod waling weavers on opposite sides of the basket, butts first. Wale the rods around the basket to their tips, passing over the butts of the alternate set. Be careful to keep the corner stakes parallel. Tap down the weave with the rapping iron when the waling is complete.

Step 10. Lay down a trac border (*see* Chapter 7). On this basket, each of the border rods passes behind two stakes, then in front of two and finally behind one stake. The tips of the border rods are left on the outside of the basket and trimmed off when the border is complete. Both the main upright and the bye stake were bent down together on each stroke to give a double trac border.

Try to keep the shape of the corner as you lay down the border rods and leave sufficient space under the first rods you bend down for the last border rods to pass under when you come to the finish. Trim off the rest of the uprights and any tips and butts from around the basket.

Project 8: Framework Willow and Hazel Platter

This free-form framework platter is made by joining the forks of two hazel branches and weaving between them with commercially grown brown willow and the occasional hazel stem. It is a good introduction to some of the principles used in framework without involving the use of skeining or accurate measurements of ribs and frames, which can both be tricky when first attempting framework. The basket is relatively quick to make and could be used for a variety of purposes, from the dining table, to displaying stones and shells collected on the beach. The size of the basket will vary with the size and width of the hazel branches. The estimates for the materials given below are, therefore, specific to the basket illustrated and you should use them only as a general guide for your own basket. Remember when selecting the branches for the frame and ribs that they still need to be thicker than your planned weavers. The random nature of this basket is one of its most attractive features, every one will turn out differently!

Materials

- Two small, forked hazel branches, for the main frame.
- The main stem of each fork on the basket was approximately 1.5cm (½ inch) in diameter and each of the two side-stems was approximately 1cm across at the point it leaves the main stem. Each side-stem was 40–50cm (16–20 inches) long.
- Four hazel sticks 40cm (14–15 inches) long, for the ribs (or willow rods).
- The rib sticks should be slightly thinner than the side-stems of the main branches.
- Four thin hazel stems for occasional weavers.
- Twenty to thirty fine 90 cm (3ft) brown willow rods, for the main weaving.

Method

Step 1. Soak and mellow all the willow rods.

Step 2. Join the hazel forks together and form the shape you desire by twisting the side-stems of one fork around the side stems of the other, letting the tips ends of the side-shoots rest against the butt of the main stem opposite. The slight dish shape of the basket is formed mainly by the ribs but shaping a slight upward curve when twisting the two main forks together will help to accentuate it.

Joining the forks and weaving the first rods.

Step 3. Select the rods prepared for weaving. Just as in any other piece of framework, the basket is woven from both ends at once and gradually worked in towards the middle. Begin at one end by slipping the butt end of a rod into the twist of the side-branches close to where the branch forks. Wrap the rod around the side-shoots in a figure-of-eight until the tip of the rod is reached. Repeat at the fork on the opposite end of the frame.

Step 4. Slype and cram the butts of the second rods into one of the pockets left by the figure-of-eights at each end and continue to weave back and forth over the outer frame until the tips of the second rods are reached.

Step 5. The first ribs are now added. Cut two of the rib sticks so that when they are inserted they will add depth to the frame. Slype the sticks on the back (so that the slype will not be seen on the top side of the basket), and insert one each, slype down, into the pockets left at each end by the weaving.

Step 6. To complete the basket, follow the method for weaving and adding the remaining ribs as described in Chapter 9. Add in the hazel weaving rods wherever you think they will look most attractive and try to keep some depth with the ribs, as this basket has a tendency to flatten out.

On this basket, I have used a crammed start for all the butts of the weavers instead of laying them along the central ribs, however, this is purely an aesthetic and not a structural choice. Once you have finished the weaving trim off any protruding ends,

Opposite: Free form platter.

Project 9: Framework Seagrass Basket

This frame basket is made using a combination of thick willow and seagrass cord. I have also used a thick laurel rod as the part of the main hoop, which forms the handle bow, but the hoop could just as easily be made entirely out of willow. The method of weaving the cord onto the frame is no different to weaving on a set of willow rods. Only the method of joining in new lengths of material varies.

Follow the instructions given in Chapter 9 when making up the hoops and ribs. I recommend that you glance through the whole of Chapter 9 in order to gleen some general guidance on weaving other parts of the basket. The ribs were all made the same size when shaping them but were cut down to size prior to insertion into the weave. The width of the rim on the small hoop has been widened with a split willow rod and skeining to give the rim of the basket more bulk after it has been woven. However, there is no reason why you can't leave it as a single rod hoop, which will give it a thinner effect.

Opposite: Seagrass basket.

Attached split rods to widen the hoop.

Materials

- One or two hanks of seagrass, for the weaving.
- Two oval hoops, for the main frame: one of approximately 25 x 15cm (10 x 5 inches) and the other approximately 40 x 30cm (16 x 12 inches)
- One thick willow rod for widening the width of the small hoop.
- Approximately six to ten soaked willow rods for making skeins to tie the hoops and the eyes of God.
- Eighteen thick 180cm (6ft) willow rods, for the ribs. (Bend the butts of the rods to give them the same shape as the curve on the large hoop.)

Method

Step 1. Soak, mellow and shape all the rods for the hoops and ribs and leave them to dry. Make a bundle of skeins with the set of rods reserved for the purpose. After the hoops have dried, select the rods reserved for the main hoop and skein them together.

Step 2. To thicken the width of the small hoop, split a thick willow rod in half right along its length and taper the inside of the butt ends. Starting with the butt end, attach the whole length of the split rod to the outside circumference of the hoop with a skein. Beginning on the opposite side to where the first tapered rod started, attach and skein the other

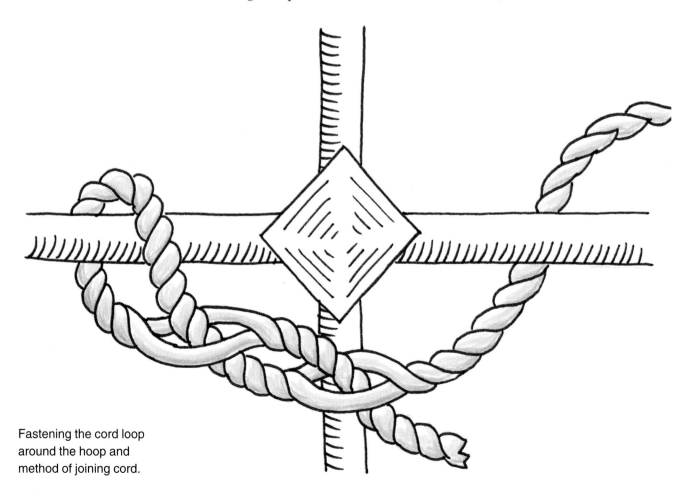

Fastening the cord loop around the hoop and method of joining cord.

split rod to the inside circumference of the hoop. Trim off any loose ends.

Step 3. With the larger hoop on the inside, lash the two hoops together at right angles with an eye of God tie.

Step 4. Unravel a few meters of seagrass from the hank and wind it into a ball, or a smaller hank, to make the cord easier to manage whilst weaving. Loop one end of the cord around the horizontal hoop to the left or right of the God's eye. Twist open a gap in the cord and thread the end through. Repeat and pull the cord tight so that it hugs the hoop. Threading the seagrass like this is the method used to join new pieces of cord in each time a length runs out. Weave the seagrass back and forth around the horizontal and vertical hoop until 3–4 cm of weaving has been completed. repeat on the other side of the frame.

Step 5. Select four rods reserved for the ribs. Cut them to length and slype the ends on the inside, so that when the tips of the slypes are inserted into the pockets left by the weaving, two of them will be slightly longer than the depth of the vertical hoop. The aim is to ensure that the basket rests on the outer ribs and not the central hoop. Cut the other two to length, so that they will lie half-way up the height of the basket. Insert these ribs into the pockets left by the weaving on either side of the main hoop.

The main hoop and the first two sets of ribs define the shape of this basket and all the ribs that remain to be inserted will follow the line indicated by these ribs. This basket does not bow out but has vertical sides and this should be taken into account when cutting the remaining ribs to length.

Step 6. Weave in and out of these ribs, as well as around the main vertical and horizontal axes, and repeat on the other side of the basket. Gradually add more pairs of measured and slyped ribs into the base and siding of the basket when appropriate pockets emerge in the weaving. Try to get all the ribs in as soon as possible and at points where they will give the weave an even spacing. Weave around all the new and old ribs individually as new ones are inserted and join in new lengths of cord, using the method described above.

Step 7. Once two or three pairs of ribs have been inserted, you will need to begin packing the cord to straighten out the line of weaving, so that the two blocks of weaving cord meet at the same point in the middle of the basket. Pack with the cord back and forth in between all the ribs at both ends of the basket, wrapping around the main horizontal hoop only intermittently until the lines of weaving are straight.

Step 8. Once all the ribs have been added and the lines of weaving on both sides of the basket are straight, finish the weaving by randing back and forth around the main hoops and the ribs until the gap in the middle of the basket is filled. Use the bodkin to assist you to weave the last couple of rows. Join the two ends of the weaving cord in the same way as you joined all the other lengths of cord together, using the method described above. Trim any protruding ends at the joins and any frayed parts of the cord with a pair of scissors.

Glossary

The following glossary is meant as a reference for all the specific terms used in this book. It also includes an explanation of some words that you may find used elsewhere on your forays into basketry.

BACK: The convex or outside curve of a rod.

BASKET: The generic word for a receptacle or vessel, usually made from a variety of woods and grasses.

BELLY: The concave or inside curve of a rod.

BILLHOOK: A slashing tool, used traditionally in the basketmaking industry to cut the willow crop.

BLACK: A type of processed, seasoned willow, which has been steamed, giving the bark a dark sheen.

BODKIN: A sharp conically-shaped tool, used for opening up the weave.

BOLT: A commercially prepared bundle of willow of one length and standard width.

BORDER: The strong decorative rim on the edges of a basket.

BOTTOM: A word often used to describe the base of a basket.

BOW: A sharply crescent, thick stick used to make handles or hoops for framework. A word also used to describe the direction of the flow in the shape of a basket.

BUFF: Used to describe willow that has been boiled and stripped, rendering it a light brown/orange colour.

BUNDLE: A word used interchangeably with BOLT.

BUTT: The thick end of a rod.

BROWN: Used to describe untreated, unstripped willow.

BYE STAKE: An extra stake inserted next to the existing upright in the upsett.

CANE: A material used for basketry and chair-seating imported from South East Asia.

CHASING: Used to describe the simultaneous use of two or more sets of weavers, each row overlapping the other.

CLEAVE: Used to describe the process of splitting rods along their length. It is also the name of a basketry tool designed for this purpose.

CLING/CLUNG: To half-dry. The condition of rods when they are half dried.

COILED WORK: A method of making baskets by stitching together a spiral of core material.

COMMANDER: A large iron tool used to straighten out kinks and bends in willow rods.

COPPICING: The process off cutting back willow and hazel, for example, in order to prompt a greater growth of shoots for cropping in following years.

CRAMMING OFF: A method of finishing a border without threading the uprights away. The upright is trimmed and tapped into the top of the border.

DRAWKNIFE: A green-woodworking tool used to shave wood and bark.

ENGLISH RAND: A weave that uses one rod at a time to work up the siding.

FITCH: A tight line of single weaving, which allows skeletal gaps to be left in the basket. It looks similar to reverse pairing.

FLOW: Used to described the lean of the uprights when shaping the basket.

FOOT BORDER: A border added to the bottom of the basket adding extra strength. It can be replaced when worn out.

FOLLOW-ON BORDER: A decorative additional border that uses the tips of the rods used to lay down the first border.

FRENCH RAND: A side weave that rands with all the rods simultaneously.

FRENCH SLEW: Uses the same techniques as ordinary randing but using two rods at once.

GREEN: The condition of material when it has first been cut. Very heavy and retaining much moisture.

GRINS: Gaps in handle wrapping.

HANDKNIFE: Used frequently through-out the basketmaking process, e.g. slyping, skeining, splitting rods.

HANDLES: The means by which a basket is picked up! They can be made in many ways and are either functional or decorative. Or both!

HEDGEROW: Materials that have not been specifically grown for the purpose of basketmaking.

HOLT: A willow bed coppiced for basketmaking.

HOOP: A simple device made of willow or string, and used to keep the uprights in position until the first rounds of weaving have been put on.

JOIN: The specific method of extending the length of a weaver. The type of join used varies with its position on the basket and the weave being used.

KINK: A method of bending a rod without snapping it. Useful when deliberately made but also easy to make by accident!

LAPBOARD: A simply designed work surface on which to make a basket. One end rests in the lap, one on the floor.

LAPPING: A skein of willow or cane that is used to wrap handles.

LASHING: Describes the use and weave of a skein when used to join the hoops of framework.

LEADER: An interwoven rod or skein used to help secure the lapping on handles.

LINER: A stick inserted into the upsett on handled baskets. When removed it leaves a space for the handle bow.

MELLOWING: Leaving willow rods in a damp cloth to allow moisture to penetrate right through the rod and render it more pliable.

NICK: A small rut cut into a stick, usually to prevent a weaving rod from slipping.

OSIER: A regional name to describe willows that are specifically grown for basketmaking.

OVAL: Describes the shape of a basket, as defined by its base.

PACKING: A section of weave that raises part or all of a side in height. It is used in items such as display baskets.

PAIRING: A simple weave using two rods at once. It is usually used only on bases.

PEG: A small wooden wedge used to secure handle bows in place.

PICKING-KNIFE: A handknife used to trim off excess weaving material.

PICK OFF: The process of trimming off the protruding ends of weaving material once a basket is finished.

PIECE-IN: Joining in a new piece of material after the previous one has run out.

PLAIT: A method of weaving the border. A decorative addition to handle wraps. Also a way of weaving rush and straw.

PLANK: A traditional sitting bench used in conjunction with the lapboard.

POLLARDING: Trimming trees at trunk, as opposed to ground level. The resulting rods can be used in some parts of basketmaking.

PRICKING-UP/PRICKING-DOWN: Bending the uprights into position, e.g. prior to putting on the upsett or laying down the border.

PRUNING SAW: Variously shaped garden handsaw. Use for cutting sticks that are too thick for secateurs.

RAFFIA: Leaf bast of the raphia palm. It is available in very long lengths and is often used in coiled work.

RAGGED: The rough edges left on the butts of willow after it has been harvested. They should be trimmed off.

RANDING: The simplest of all weaves, using one rod at time.

RANDOM WEAVE: A weave that has no standard strokes or rigid formula.

RAPPING IRON: A heavy flat hand-tool used for tapping down the weave.

REVERSE PAIRING: Similar to ordinary pairing but the weavers are held at the back, instead of the front of the work. It is usually used in conjunction with ordinary pairing on oval bases.

RIBBED: An alternative description of frame basketry.

RIVING: Splitting wood along its grain.

ROD: Usually used to describe a length of young willow when used in a basket.

ROD BORDER: A commonly used bordering technique which has several variants.

ROPE HANDLE: A handle that has been wrapped with fine rods.

ROUND: Describes the shape of a basket, as defined by its base.

RUSHWORK: The use of varieties of rush for baskets and chair-seating.

SALIX: The genus of willows.

SCALLOMING: A method for cutting the butt of a willow rod, allowing it to be attached to a hoop.

SCREWBLOCK: A device used for holding the base sticks of squarework in position while weaving.

SEAGRASS: Twisted sedge or coarse grass, it is imported from the Far East.

SECATEURS: Variously shaped pruning shears, commonly used instead of a picking-knife in modern basketry.

SHAVE: One of the tools used in making skeins.

SIDING: The vertical area of weave on a basket.

SKEIN: A ribbon of willow used to make part or all of a basket.

SLATH: The cross of sticks at the base of a basket.

SLEWING: A randing weave that chases groups of parallel weavers around the basket.

SLIT: A split made in the base sticks to allow further construction of the slath.

SLYPE: A taper put on the butt of a rod with a knife or secateurs. It eases its insertion into the weave.

SPLINT: A strip of riven and shaved wood used in basketmaking.

SQUAREWORK: Used to describe the shape of a basket, as defined by the angles on its base.

STAKE: A thick rod used to form the siding framework of a basket. Sometimes used interchangeably with UPRIGHT

STRAW-WORK: Traditional method of working straw to make baskets and corn dollies.

STROKE: A single movement in the process of weaving.

STUFF: A word used to describe basketmaking material

TIP: The thin top end of a rod.

TRAC BORDER: A simple narrow border usually seen on lightweight baskets or lidded work.

TRUNK WALE: A type of thick waling used to form a ledge for a lid to rest on.

UPRIGHT: A word used to describe the vertical stakes on the side of a basket. Also a tool used for skeining

UPSETT: The first two or three rounds of waling at the bottom of a basket.

WALING: A very strong weave that simultaneously uses a minimum of three rods. It is used at frequent intervals on most baskets.

WEATHER: Allowing material to season or 'cling' slightly.

WEAVER: A rod used for weaving in basketmaking.

WEIGHT: Stabilizes the basket whilst it is being worked.

WHITE: Stripped, unprocessed willow.

WITHY: A regional word for a willow rod.

Further Reading

Abbott, M., *Green Woodwork: Working Wood the Natural Way* (The Guild of Mastercraftsmen, 1989)

Barratt, O.E., *Rushwork* (Dryad Press) Butcher, M., *Willow Work* (Dryad Press, 1986)

Finley, J.T., *Rib Baskets* (Schiffer Publishing Ltd., 1987)

Gabriel, S. and Goymer, S., *The Complete Book of Basketry Techniques* (David & Charles, 1991)

Harding, P. and Tomblin, G., *How to Identify Trees* (Collins, 1996)

Hessayon, Dr D.G., *The Tree and Shrub Expert* (Expert Books, 1994)

Jensen, E., *Baskets from Nature's Bounty* (Interweave Press, 1991)

Lambert, F., *Tools and Devices for Coppice Crafts* (Evan Brothers, 1957)

Langsner, D., *Green Woodworking: A Hands-On Approach* (Lark Books, 1995)

Law, W., Nash, R. and Taylor, C., *Appalachian White Oak Basketmaking* (University of Tennessee Press, 1991)

Lee, B., *British Naturalists' Association Guide to Fields, Farms and Hedgerow* (The Crowood Press, 1985)

Maynard, B., *Modern Basketry Techniques* (Batsford, 1989)

Mowat, L., Morphy, H. and Dransart, P., *Basketmakers: Meaning and Form in Native American Baskets* (Pitt Rivers Museum, 1992)

Rossbach, E., *Baskets as Textile Art* (Studio Vista, 1974)

Vaughan, S., *Handmade Baskets from Nature's Colourful Materials* (Search Press, 1994)

W.I. Books Ltd., *The Women's Institute Book of Country Crafts* (Chancellor Press, 1994)

Wilkinson, J., *Willow Growing and Propagation* (Available from author, 1998).

INTERNET REFERENCE

Investigating the subjects of both basketmaking and weaving on the Internet can prove extremely fruitful. Here are just a couple of useful addresses:

Weave – Network
HTT:// WWW. WEAVENET.COM

General Basketry Information
HTTP://WWW.ULSTER.NET-ABEEBE/BASKET.HTML

Useful Addresses

ASSOCIATIONS

Argyll Green-Woodworkers Association, c/o A & BCT, Tigh Mhicleoid, Lochnell St, Lochgilphead, Argyll. Scotland.

Association of Michigan Basketmakers, Nancy Carlson, 1258 South Drive, Mt. Pleasant, MI 48858, USA.

Basketry Network, Lori Bond, 1850 Bloor St. E.106, Mississauga, Ontario, L4X IT3, Canada

The Basketmakers' Association, Membership: Sally Goymer, 37 Mendip Rd, Cheltenham, Glos., England, GL52 5EB.

Basketmakers of Victoria, P.O. Box 1067, East Campberwell 3126, Australia.

Basketweavers' Guild – Mid West, Frederick Kogler (Director), 1637 Alan Court, West St. Paul, MN 55118 – 3802, USA.

Coppice Association North West, c/o Cumbria Broadleaves, Rayrigg Meadow, Bowness on Windermere, Cumbria, England, LA23 1BP.

Greenwood Trust, Station Rd, Coalbrookdale, Telford, Shropshire, England, TF8 7DR.

Maine Indian Basketmakers Alliance, P.O. Box 3253, Old Town, ME 04468, USA.

National Small Woods Association, Hall Farm House, Preston Capes, Northants, England, NN11 6TA.

Scottish Basketmakers' Circle, c/o: Graham Glanville, Backbraes, Whithorn, Newton Stewart, Scotland, DG8 8DZ.

SUPPLIERS

Cane, Cord, Tools and Dyes

F. Aldous Ltd., P.O. Box 135, 37 Lever St, Manchester 1, England, M60 1UX.

Ashill Colour Studio, Jenny Dean, Boundary Cottage, 172 Clifton Rd, Shefford, Beds, England, SG17 5AH.

Berrycraft Acadia, Swansbrook Lane, Horam, Heathfield, East Sussex, England, TN21 OLD.

The Cane Store, 207 Blackstock Rd, Highbury Vale, London, England.

M. & R. Dyes, Carters, Station Rd, Wickham Bishops, Withham, Essex, England, CM8 3JB.

D.F. Ellwood & Son, Rope & Twine Manufacture, Station Works, Kendall, Cumbria, England, LA9 6HP.

J. Excell, The Cane Workshop, The Gospel Hall, Westport, Langport, Somerset. England.

The H. H. Perkins Co., Basketry Supplies & Dyes, 10 South Bradley Rd, Woodbridge, Conneticut, 06525, USA.

Woodland Craft Supplies, Windsors Cottage, Felixtowe Ferry, Suffolk, England, IP11 9RZ.

Rushes

T. Arnold, Wildcroft, Holywell, St. Ives, Huntingdon, Cambridgeshire, England, PE17 3TG.

I. & J. L. Brown Ltd., 58 Commercial Rd, Hereford, England, HR1 2BP.

Country Chairmen, Home Farm, School Rd, Ardington, Nr. Wantage, Oxfordshire, England.

J. Excell, The Cane Workshop, The Gospell Hall, Westport, Langport, Somerset, England.

F. Irons, Keepers Lodge, Pound Lane, Kimbolton, Cambridgeshire, England, PE18 0HR.

Jacobs, Young and Westbury Ltd., Bridge Rd., Haywards Heath, West Sussex, England, HR16 1TZ.

Straw

D. Butler, Woolley Green Farm, Braishfield Romsey, Hants. England.

G.A. Liddle, Foxholes Farm, Hanbury, Burton-upon-Trent, England, DE13 8TQ.

C. Payne, 2 Stoneyrock Cottage, Nags Head Lane, Great Missenden, Buckinghamshire, England.

Willow Plants

Christies Tree Nursery, Christie Elite, Forress, Moray, Scotland, IV36 OTW.

S. Pickup, The Willow Bank, Y Fron, Llawr-y-Glynn, Caersws, Powys, Wales, SY17 5RT.

Willows

E. Batty, Glebe Farm, Norwell, Newark, Nottinghamshire, England.

Coate & Sons, Meare Green Court, Stoke St., Gregory, Nr. Taunton, Somerset, England.

Derham Bros., Foster's Farm, North Curry, Taunton, Somerset, England.

English Basketry Willows, RFD1, Box 124a, Dept. A, South New Berlin, New York, 13843, USA.

R. & R. Hector, 18 Windmill Hill, North Curry, Nr. Taunton, Somerset, England.

Jacobs, Young and Westbury Ltd., Bridge Rd., Haywards Heath, West Sussex, England, HR16 1TZ.

Lock Leaze, Kings Episcopy, Martock, Somerset, England.

C. Mollart, Broadwater Farm, Ossington, Newark, Nottinghamshire, England. Royalwood Ltd., 517 Woodville Rd, Mansfield, Ohio, 44907, USA.

Stoke Willows, Dark Lane, Stoke St., Gregory, Nr. Taunton, Somerset, England.

Walters Ltd., Mountain Rd, Washington Island, 54246, USA.

CONTRIBUTING BASKETMAKERS

Lizzie Farey, 8 Threave Road, Rhonehouse, Castle Douglas, Scotland, DG7 1SA.

Graham Glanville, Backbraes, Whithorn, Newton Stewart, Scotland, DG8 8DZ.

Trevor Leat, The Hill, Balmaclellan, Castle Douglas, Scotland, DG7 3PW.

Georgia Crook, Feorlin Cottage, Carsaig, Isle of Mull, Argyll, PA70 6ND.

Index

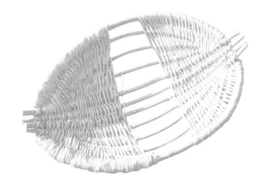